Seventh Century Man

Muslims in search of identity in the Twenty First century.

Michael Nimier, PhD (Lond.)

A Sponsored Publication of E-Learning International incorporating AUOL the American University of London.

First published in Great Britain by:
SatinPublishing.co.uk

All paper used in the printing of this book has been made from wood grown in managed, sustainable forests.

ISBN-13: 978-1978236431
ISBN-10: 1978236433

Printed and bound in the UK

A catalogue record of this book is available from the British Library

Cover design by: designforwriters.com

About the author

Dr. Michael Nimier started his undergraduate studies at the Faculty of Pharmacy, Universita' di Roma-Italy and subsequently took up a scholarship to pursue his area of interest in political science at the School of Oriental and African Studies, University of London. He was awarded an MA in Area Studies (Middle East) and a PhD in Politics.

He has been involved in International Education as a professor of Politics , International Relations , and Islamic Government for many years. He has had a number of articles published in journals and newspapers around the world.   This is his third book.

A multilingual Nimier is also fluent in Arabic

Website : www.michaelnimier.com

Twitter : https://twitter.com/MichaelNimier

Veritas vos Liberabit

PART 1

Islamic Terror and the Future of Western Civilization

In Barcelona's Las Ramblas Avenue in the afternoon of Thursday August 13 2017, a Muslim terrorist shouting Allahu Akbar ploughed his van into an unsuspecting crowd enjoying an afternoon promenade in the balmy sunshine, killing 13 people and injuring more than a hundred. On June the 3rd in London Bridge, another Muslim terrorist killed eight people and injured many others.

These atrocities have become a regular feature of our daily life in Europe. On May the 22, 2017 in the Manchester Arena 23 teens and young people were slaughtered while attending a concert by the singer Ariana Grande. In Stockholm April 7, Paris April 20th and many more similar atrocities.

We recoil with shock, feel the pain, shed the tears, light the candles, hold our vigils, and repeat the well-rehearsed mantra "we are not afraid", "we are all Charlie Hebdo" and so on. In a day or two amnesia kicks in and we revert to our daily life with the explanation that the terrorists must not win.

Muslim terror attacks are our new normal. We have factored them into our very existence; we expect them and when they do come, we are not surprised. Regularity desensitized us, making us lose our instinct for outrage. Our reaction has become mute and ineffectual.

We always start with the question "why do they hate us?" followed by "and as they clearly do, why do they choose to live amongst us?". I have answered these questions on a number of occasions in my other blogs.

Suffice to say that whilst many explanations are given, the root of it lies in the Islamic scriptures particularly in the Quran, the edifice upon which the religion Islam is constructed.

This begs the all-important question, is immigration important for the continued overall growth of European societies? The answer is both Yes and No! Yes, if the immigrants assimilate in their new host countries, in other words if they like and respect the societies and the culture they choose to live in. In the 16th and 17th centuries, to give but one example French Protestant Huguenots fled religious persecution in their country and sought refuge in the UK mostly in East London. They are now fully assimilated and form an important component of British society. Jews who migrated to Britain over many decades are now well integrated citizens who have made great contributions to British culture and way of life. There are many such examples in most European nations.

What distinguishes those new arrivals is that they are mostly inter-European migrants. Whether they are

Poles, Irish, Spanish or even Russians, they share with their host countries a common European Judeo-Christian heritage, they come with no hidden agendas and more importantly they owe no allegiance nor loyalty to any external religious or political higher authority.

In a time of ageing populations in almost all European nations as well as a declining birth rate, inter-European movement of people from countries with high unemployment to countries requiring labour should be encouraged. In every single European country, the birth rate is well below the crucial 2.1 level. Let us refer to this movement of citizens within Europe as internal migration as opposed to international migration from outside the European Union.

The post Brexit Europe should aim to stop the creeping incursion of illiberal and authoritarian ideologies disguised as "religions" or "cultures" into the continent's liberal and democratic way of life. In most European nations, adherence to liberal values has resulted in the growth of illiberal values. To put it differently our free and liberal societies began to tolerate the intolerant. If this trend is not stopped its long-term consequences will be catastrophic for the face of Europe as we and our ancestors have known it. Europe's tolerance and support of the wrongly called ideal of multi-culturalism has resulted in the growth of a continent of multi-faithism. In most instances, International migrants have failed and in many cases chosen not to – integrate in their host nations. In other cases, they displayed non-acceptance and/or blatant hostility towards the hosts' values. A considerable number aggregated in ghettos where they set up schools indoctrinating their young ones in the culture of their home countries.

The revival of a religious narrative in many European nations as an inevitable backlash to the growth of alien religiosity amidst secular Europeans, is another disturbing phenomenon. It took Europe five hundred years of evolution to reach this stage of separation of state and religion.

If not halted immediately the consequence of continued International immigration to Europe will have a severe impact on European civilization. As Douglas Murray puts in in his excellent book "The Strange Death of Europe".

"Demographic studies show ethnic Swedes becoming a minority in Sweden within the lifespan of most people currently alive, which raises the fascinating question of whether Swedish identity has any chance of surviving this generation. This question will also have to be faced by every other Western European country".

Bleak Future?

The recent waves of immigration were the principle (albeit unspoken) cause of Brexit and the rise of right wing nationalist parties in most European states. Islamic violence shocked the American people as well resulting in the victory of Donald Trump.

Inaction by the centrist governments in Europe is political nihilism. If European leaders, subdued by the tyranny of guilt and history continue to gloss over the caldron that is bubbling on the continent public outrage at the changing demographic landscape of the continent will erupt into extremism and violent nationalism. Europeans, naively considered Islamic new comers as no different from other migrants to the continent, eager to integrate in a superior culture and become active part of it. What they did not imagine is that a considerable number of the Muslim newcomers didn't want to integrate but to dominate. The era of dog eats dog at the height of the Weimar Republic will raise its nasty head again if the political status quo is not changed. Seeking shelter in extremism will be the only shelter available to the disaffected masses. In the words of Tony Blankley "The day is upon us when the West will have to decide which it values more: granting European rights and tolerance to those who wish to destroy us, or the survival of Western civilization".

In order to make sure that this nightmare scenario does not occur two overarching objectives must be fulfilled.

- *A strong European Union ultimately leading to the establishment of the UNITED STATES OF EUROPE with unhindered internal movement of its citizens and a securely protected external border.*

- *A stop to all immigration from outside the European continent except for persecuted members of minorities who do not adhere to values in conflict with European values. This excludes Turkey, a non-European Islamic nation tittering on the precipice of dictatorship whose overall cultural and political values are in stark contrast to European civilization. Its application for membership to the European Union should be sent back immediately.*

Anything short of the above will not satisfy the majority of Europeans.

Grooming

No one becomes a murdering terrorist overnight. But young men who blow themselves up to take with them as many people as possible, or draw a knife and slit the throat of an innocent unsuspecting priest at the height of performing his mass, or drive a vehicle and run over entire families enjoying a day out on the Promenade des Anglais in Nice-France or other similar atrocities, do have one thing in common.

They are true Muslim Puritans who fulfil the commands of Allah as literally dictated in the Quran and in Muslim scriptures.

Their victims too have one thing in common. They are all *Kuffar*, infidels who continue to resist Islam's Daawa (call, summons,) to join the "pure" religion (*al din al Haneef*) and by doing so have sealed their own fate.

Quran

The Quran is the first and most important instrument of grooming. A child reading the Quran at an early age will inevitably see the extent of hatred heaped on all non-Muslims on whom, in the words of Sam Harris, Allah is in the process of "mocking," "cursing," "shaming," "punishing," "scourging," "judging," "burning," "annihilating," "not forgiving," and "not reprieving."

A child engrossed in the Quran will learn that Allah *prolongs the life and prosperity of the infidels so that they may continue heaping sin upon sin upon themselves and all the more richly deserve the torments that await them beyond the grave.*

On almost every page of the Quran vulnerable children are being groomed for conflict with the infidels (the Kuffar).

Also on almost every page, the seeds of hatred are being planted. The link between Islam and violence is there for every child to absorb. And when the child is in life's early stages of innocence and development the foundation for grooming are being laid. A child will also begin to absorb the degree of trickery and deviousness of the narrative which will help him in later life explain and justify acts of terror against non-Muslims.

The child will have learnt that the Kuffar are indispensable and that they are nothing more than fuel for the eternal fires of Allah's justice.

Madrassa

As soon as a Muslim child is of a nursery or elementary school age he/she is sent to a Madrassa where the second important stage of grooming takes place.

Madrassas are the most common type of school for religious instruction at the elementary level in the Islamic world. These schools specialize in the teaching of Qur'anic texts which children are trained to learn by heart.

Islamic instruction at the Madrassa is combined with anti-Western propaganda. In most instances the Madrassas are places where terrorists are formed ideologically.

These centuries-old Islamic religious institutions came into closer focus after the terrorist attacks of September 11, 2011, when experts suspected that Madrassas teaching Islamic extremism were tied to al-Qaeda and other terrorist organizations, fermenting anti-Western propaganda and fostering hatred toward the West in general.

Unquestionably in recent years, there has been a rise in the number of religious schools in the Islamic world, and particularly of schools dominated by the more fundamentalist Wahhabi and Salafi strains of Islam.

The schools are mostly funded by Saudi Arabia, considered to be the major exporter of finance and Wahhabi ideology to the world. In Pakistan to give but one example about 24,000 Madrassas are funded by Saudi Arabia which has "unleashed a tsunami of

money to export intolerance", as stated recently by a
top American senator.

*"It would be troublesome but perhaps acceptable
for the House of Saud to promote the intolerant and
extremist Wahhabi creed just domestically. But,
unfortunately, for decades the Saudis have also
lavishly financed its propagation abroad. Exact
numbers are not known, but it is thought that more
than $100 billion have been spent on exporting
fanatical Wahhabism to various much poorer Muslim
nations worldwide over the past three decades. It
might well be twice that number. By comparison, the
Soviets spent about $7 billion spreading communism
worldwide in the 70 years from 1921 and 1991."*

Other donors include Qatar who through its
mouthpiece Aljazeera Arabic conducts a relentless
campaign of extreme Islamic propaganda and brain
washing.

Family

Children are increasingly being "radicalised in
their bedrooms" The role of Muslim families in
grooming a future terrorist is often under estimated.
In tribal societies, as in the Middle East in general
parents exercise greater influence on their children.
Those parents who hold literalist views of the Islamic
scriptures particularly the Quran will pass on these

views to their offspring whether consciously or unconsciously.

Within the family milieu children will be exposed to the violent, anti-Western extremist views and rhetoric of their parents. This will inevitably lead to the development of a distorted world view in the child in which extremist ideology seems the norm. Within such family's children are being individually groomed and radicalized by their parents whilst the parents themselves are often unaware of what is going on. Gradually they become victims of brain washing and insidious radicalization. This constitutes as important a layer of grooming as the Quran.

A common feature of this form of subtle grooming is that the child does not recognise the exploitative nature of what is happening and does not see himself as victim of exploitation. The parents also may have inadvertently expedited this process of grooming by reinforcing the narrative already learnt in the Quran, the Madrassas, the local mosques and on the internet.

In the progress of grooming parents will not take too much notice of changes in the child's character and demeanour. Expressing intolerant views towards non-Muslims, espousing verbal support for illegal organizations which are lauded by the parents and often referred to "real Muslims", "true Mujahids in Allah's cause" are viewed with satisfaction by

parents who feel they have succeeded in their mission
to bring up their children as "good Muslims". The
child's family continues to be supportive of their
child's views and behaviour regardless of how
extremists they appear to be.

*Children as young as seven have been identified as
being groomed for terrorism, with some already
talking about become suicide bombers. In the UK
around 10 primary school pupils, aged between seven
and 10, have been referred to a Government scheme
to help combat the radicalisation of youngsters. (the
Telegraph Monday 19 June 2017) one child wrote in
his school book: "I want to be a suicide bomber" (the
telegraph Monday 19 June 2017).*

Mosque

Recently released Guantanamo files revealed that
35 Jihadists were groomed for terrorism at British
mosques before being sent to fight against the West.

Numerous mosques in Western nations have
become an international haven for extremists who in
many instances enjoyed state benefits while being
trained for terrorism, the leaked documents show.

The files point to the crucial role of mosque
preachers in indoctrinating extremists. U.S.
intelligence officers describe the notorious Finsbury
Park mosque in North London, as a haven for Islamic

extremists and "an attack planning and propaganda production base'.

Internet

Terrorism on the Internet extends far beyond Web sites directly operated or controlled by terrorist organizations.

Their supporters and sympathizers are increasingly taking advantage of all the tools available on the Web. "The proliferation of blogs has been exponential."

The Internet appeals to terrorists for the same reasons it attracts everyone else: It's inexpensive, easily accessible, it's anonymous, has little or no regulation, is interactive, allows for multimedia content and the potential audience is huge.

"One of the things that IS (Islamic State) has been incredibly successful at has been using the internet and social networking for the dissemination of their own propaganda."

The use of the Internet to spawn hate sites and recruit advocates for hate began as early as the 1990s. Since then hundreds of hate sites and other websites. advocating terror have been developed.

Gabriel Weimann, a professor of communication at Haifa University in Israel and a terrorism researcher monitors more than 7,000 such sites.

"You can walk into an Internet café, enter a chat room or Web site, download instructions to make a bomb, and no one can find you," says Weimann. "They can trace you all the way down to the computer terminal, but by then you'll already be gone."

The University of Arizona's "Dark Web" project, which tracks terrorist and extremist content in cyberspace, estimates there are roughly 50,000 such Web sites, discussion forums, chat rooms, blogs, Yahoo user groups, video-sharing sites, social networking sites and virtual worlds. They help to distribute content — such as videos of beheadings and suicide attacks, speeches by terrorist leaders and training manuals — that may originate on just a few hundred sites.

Terrorist groups use the Internet for research and communication and training The Sept. 11, 2001, terrorists who attacked the World Trade Centre and the Pentagon used the Internet to research flight schools, coordinate their actions through e-mail and gather flight information. The Global Islamic Media Front, a propaganda arm of al Qaeda, issued a series of 19 training lessons in 2003 covering topics like security, physical training, weapons and explosives.

The internet is also used for fundraising: In 1997, the rebel Tamil Tigers in Sri Lanka stole user IDs and passwords from faculty at Britain's Sheffield University and used the e-mail accounts to send out messages asking for donations.

The use of the Internet for recruitment and radicalization is particularly worrisome. The Internet is where "the gas meets the flame," says Evan F. Kohlmann, a senior investigator with the NEFA Foundation, a New York-based terrorism research organization. The internet provides the medium where would-be megalomaniacs can try and recruit deluded and angry young men. and magnify that anger to convince them to carry out acts of violence."

Conclusion

A question often heard and debated in academic circles and elsewhere is "Why do they hate us?" Why do they hate us to the point of killing innocent men women and children who have no quarrel with Islam and who in most probability know very little or may be even nothing about the religion? Why do they kill tourists visiting and spending money in *their* country and thus helping the economy of *their* country grow and prosper? The explanation is not political. It is not economic. It is not social.

The answer is purely religious. Muslims' hatred of non-Muslims- the Kuffar- is in their DNA. Every

Muslim who reads the Quran is born with it. Ever since the Quran was written and adopted as the holy book of Muslims, this hatred has been passed on from generation to generation over the last 1500 years.

While only a small minority of Muslims resort to terror all Muslims share a literal interpretation and total acceptance of the Quran's narrative. The only difference is that the terrorists are the puritans who take the Quran's call to "punish" the infidels literally and act on it with conviction.

From the moment the grooming starts at birth to the time a heinous act of terror is committed, the terrorist passes through a number of grooming "stations" as described above. Some pass through all the stations, others go through one or more. The influence of each station varies depending on a number of circumstances. The one thing they all have in common (justification of a future act of terror by the "apprentice" is the reference to the words of Allah as delivered to Muhammad in the Quran. The infidels are nothing more than fuel for the eternal fires of Allah's justice. As such the Quran remains the perennial and most important station in the grooming of terrorists.

Islamic Banking:
A Charade or a Scam?

Islamic banking refers to banking in accordance with Sharia (Islamic law) ostensibly with emphasis on moral and ethical values in dealings with money lending and borrowing. Sharia prohibits the payment or acceptance of interest (referred to as RIBA). Notice the use of the derogatory Arabic word RIBA, meant to describe usury (lending at extortionist price) rather than the word FA'IDA which simply means interest or the price of money.

Commercial banks as we know them today date back to the sixteenth century; there were no Muslim banks at the time nor any form of exclusively Islamic banking. The prohibition of RIBA in the Quran by Muhammad was meant for his constituents at the time mostly members of his own Qureshi tribe long before banking was even heard of. His message to the affluent members of his tribe was simple" do not take advantage of your less fortunate fellow tribesmen".

It is only in the late 20th century, in the mid-1960s to be precise, that many Islamic banks began to make an appearance to provide Muslims with this alternative basis to lending and borrowing and.to operate in accordance with the rules of Sharia known as *Fiqh al-Muamalat* (the theology of commerce). *In* 1966 the Egyptian Muslim scholar, Abu Ala Maudie wrote a treatise entitled The Economic System declaring all forms of interest to be *haram* (forbidden by Allah). In the same year a fellow Sunni, Abdullah al-Arabi, wrote the first paper about 'Islamic banking' focusing on the idea of profit sharing through a process called *Mudarabah.*

By way of an example, if someone wants a Sharia-compliant mortgage, on a $100,000 property, they can enter a transaction where the bank buys the property from the vendor (for $100,000), immediately sells it to the purchaser for, say, $200,000, but allows the purchaser to repay that amount, interest-free, for $10,000 a year for 20 years. (This is called *Murabaha*).

Another type of mortgage is structured as a joint purchase - the bank and the buyer purchase the property jointly, and the bank gradually sells out their share to the buyer (who has exclusive use of the property.) The buyer pays the bank according to a pre-determined schedule, part of which is repayment of an interest-free loan on their portion, and part of which is rent on the bank's assets. This kind of arrangement is called *Mishawaka.*

According to their Profit-Sharing Principle Islamic banks provide accounts which offer profit/loss instead of traditional accounts with pre-determined interest rates.

Misharaka and Murabaha mean the same thing - sharing- Two terms meant to add a certain aura of mystery and complexity to the pious and unsuspecting borrower whose main aim is to abide by Allah's scriptures and to avoid His threat to end up in hell" We have prepared for those among them who reject faith a grievous punishment. (Quran sura 4:161)".

The main principle sources and references of Fiqh al-Muamalat are the Qur'an followed by the Hadith (recorded sayings and actions of Prophet Muhammad).

Where solutions to banking issues cannot be found in these two sources, rulings are made on an ad hoc basis based on pronouncements/fatwas of Islamic ulama, so long as these pronouncements do not deviate from the fundamental teachings in the Qur'an.

This means if a financial product offered is deemed un-Islamic, in other words RIBA-based, then the" sin" and responsibility of that flaw lies with the Islamic Scholar who issued the decree and not with the Bank. Islamic Banks essentially work with these decrees that absolve them of any wrong-doing from a Shariah point of view.

The following are the Qur'anic *suras* (verses) most often referred to, to explain and justify objection to straightforward imposition of a pre-agreed interest. The references in the Suras below are meant for Riba and not Fa-ida.

In the Quran

- *Surat Al-Bacharach -COW- [verse 275].
  [Quran 2:275] Those who charge interest
  (referred to as RIBA-usury-) are in the same
  position as those controlled by the devil's
  influence. This is because they claim that
  usury is the same as commerce. However,
  God permits commerce, and prohibits usury.
  Thus, whoever heeds this commandment from
  his Lord, and refrains from usury, he may
  keep his past earnings, and his judgment rests
  with God. As for those who persist in usury,
  they incur Hell, wherein they abide forever.*

- *(Surah al-Rum, verse 39) That which you give
  as RIBA to increase the peoples' wealth
  increases not with God; but that which you
  give in charity, seeking the goodwill of God,
  multiplies manifold. (30:39).*

- *(Surah al-Nisa', verse 161) And for their
  taking RIBA even though it was forbidden for
  them, and their wrongful appropriation of
  other peoples' property, we have prepared for
  those among them who reject faith a grievous
  punishment. (4:161).*

- *(Surah Al 'Imran, verses 130-2) O believers,
  take not doubled and redoubled RIBA, and
  fear God so that you may prosper. Fear the*

fire which has been prepared for those who reject faith, and obey God and the Prophet so that you may receive mercy. (3:130-2).

In Hadith

- *From 'Abdallah ibn Hatzalah: The Prophet, said: "A dirham of RIBA which a man receives knowingly is worse than committing adultery thirty-six times" (Mishkat al-Masabih, Kitab al-Buyu', Bab al-RIBA on the authority of Ahmad and Daraqutni). Bayhaqi has also reported the above hadith in Shu'ab al-iman with the addition that "Hell befits him whose flesh has been nourished by the unlawful."*

- *From Abu Hurayrah: The Prophet, said: "RIBA has seventy segments, the least serious being equivalent to a man committing adultery with his own mother." (Ibn Maja).*

As Islamic banking is based on the Profit-Sharing principle the bank and the borrower become owners of the Asset/Venture for which the loan is advanced. In this" partnership" "murabaha" banks advance the money and the borrower manages the business. Both parties share in a pre-determined percentage of the profits. Worth noting that murabaha (profit sharing ribh= Arabic for profit) was not the innovation of Muslim scholars as is often claimed but the work of European Christians in the Middle Ages who gave their blessing Contractor Trinius to Christian merchants/bankers allowing them to bypass Christian rulings against Usury. It could therefore be said that Islamic banking was no more than the aping of a Christian tradition prevalent in the Middle Ages.

Global Islamic banking is on the crest of a new renaissance to be found everywhere (in the USA alone Islamic banking commands revenues of up to 4 trillion US$). This amount has everyone salivating and trying to come up with products to get a piece of this pie. The international bankers have been very active in this segment and sharia scholars have been very happy to oblige them (for a fee of course) on how to Islamize the products available in conventional financing.

These products are for ever growing and changing to please the hungry banks for the Muslims' money. They include:

1) *Tawarruq or reverse murabaha*

2) *Wa'ad (promise, refers to an obligation issued by one counterparty, to another, and whereby the promisor undertakes towards the promise to proceed with the contract. Shari's considers a promise as binding on the issuer unless an excuse (force majeure) comes forth -Wikipedia*

3) Sukuk (Islamic bonds, structured in such a way as to generate returns to investors without infringing Islamic law (that prohibits RIBA / interest)) Wikipedia

4) Sharia compliant derivates

5) Profit rate swaps

When a borrower does not consider a product or service to be sharia compliant, lawyers and sharia scholars will bang their heads together on it for a while and make it a sharia compliant product lured by the irresistible incentive of a hefty fee of course.

There will always be people who will continue to justify one product or other and have detailed fatwas and explanations how a certain transaction is sharia compliant.

Islamic finance is neither a radical concept nor a new one. Islamic finance is already being recommended as zero fractional reserve banking in the West. All the products already exist and conventional banks already carry out such transactions.

One financially positive thing that can be said about exclusively Islamic banks is that they are reticent to invest in junk bonds. However, to claim that transactions by Islamic banks have no association with interest, is a delusion many ordinary Muslim investors believe for fear of offending Allah.

Islamic Finance Loans avoid interest by theoretically having a bank buy a car or house on a Muslim's behalf, and then reselling the asset to a Muslim at an artificially inflated price over many years at 0% interest. The pricing of the payments is pegged to whatever the interest price would be plus a premium to pay for a Shariah compliance certificate from a participating Muslim theologian. The Muslim theologian is paid a fee for the certificate.

Legally speaking an Islamic Finance Loan works exactly like a conventional loan, but charged at a higher interest rate.

Similarly, in the Bond market, the Shariah compliant Sukuk bond (invented in 1990) works just like a conventional bond, but pays a lower interest rate to Muslims who feel they are not allowed to collect conventional interest payments.

In conclusion, many argue that Islamic banking is at best a charade and at worst no more than a modern-day scam taking advantage of the ambiguity around the Arabic term Riba.

Islamophobia Debunked

"Islamophobia" is a term adopted by Muslim apologists and members of the Liberal and Left wing establishment. In a supposed show of tolerance, they embrace a totalitarian ideology in its most vicious form. Western liberals have in essence sided with the Islamists fanatics betraying those who genuinely seek to reform Islam.

The net result was tarnishing the understandable fear, anger and weariness of Europeans and Americans of the incessant Muslim terror attacks and the rising hostility towards the non-Muslims host populations derisibly referred to in most Muslim scriptures as the Kuffar: infidels.

Islamophobia is a recent term that started appearing in the mid to late 1990s. It must not be confused with "xenophobia", the blanket and unjustifiable fear of the strangers.

Prior to the rise of Islamic terror, Muslim residents in Europe and America enjoyed a relatively peaceful co-existence in their host nations. Islam was viewed

as yet another addition to the religious mosaic that is
Europe and America. Most citizens in the host
nations considered Islam no differently from the way
they considered their own religions- a set of rules and
directives regulating Man's spiritual relationship with
God. There was no reason to delve deeply into the
true Islam nor to dissect its scriptures and holy book.
As such there was no discrimination against Muslims
due to their religion, or perceived religious, national,
or ethnic identity.

The onslaught of indiscriminate terror on
unsuspecting civilians changed all that. People began
to wonder why the Muslims hate us. Many scholars
began to take a serious look at the Islamic scriptures
particularly the Quan "the constitution of Islam"
resulting in rational criticism of the religion based on
historical factual evidence. This is no different from
the criticism of the tenets of other religions or
ideologies and is not an indication of bigotry or
prejudice. The European Renaissance and
Reformation would never have come into existence
had it not been for the criticism of Christianity.

The term 'Islamophobia,' is a malicious attack on
free thinking and a means of muzzling all criticism of
Islam. It must not to be equated with anti-Semitism,
racism, sexism and homophobia. These are
expressions of hostility, prejudice, and discrimination
against Jews, people of colour, women and

homosexuals for no reason other than for being who they are. They have not committed atrocities against innocent people of a different religion, race sex or sexual orientation.

The correct term to define the weariness sweeping the world because of Islamic terror and the justified reaction to it should be Islamo-Weariness or Islamo-Phatigue.

Critics of Islam are being shamed into silence for criticizing the Muslim religious tenets by calling them bigots and Islamophobes. The real aim is to shield the ideology of Islam itself from criticism. The fear of being labelled an Islamophobe is increasing thus fulfilling the objectives of those who aim at curtailing any criticism of the religion itself.

Sam Harris described Islamophobia as a "word created by fascists, & used by cowards, to manipulate morons." He added:

"Islam is not a race, ethnicity, or nationality: It's a set of ideas, Criticism of these ideas should never be confused with an animus toward people. And yet it is. I'm convinced that this is often done consciously, strategically, and quite cynically as a means of shutting down conversation on important topics."

Israeli Settlements in the West Bank: A Deal Breaker?

Demographics

The Security Council of the United Nations recently (2016) Adopted a resolution 2334 stating that Israel's establishment of settlements in Palestinian territory occupied since 1967, including East Jerusalem, have no validity in international law and is a major obstacle to the establishment of two States living side-by-side in peace and security, within internationally recognised borders.

The Council also demand that Israel immediately and completely cease all settlement activities in the occupied Palestinian territory, it underlined that it would not recognise any changes to the 4 June 1967 borders, other than those agreed by the two sides through negotiations.

The number of Israeli settlers in the West Bank currently stands at 474.000 of a total population of 4. 500.00 constituting approximately 14% of the total population. The number of Palestinian Arabs living in Israel proper is 1,800.000 of a total population of 8.000.000 constituting approximately 22% of the country's total population.

Let us for the time being imagine that peace has "broken out" between Palestine and Israel and a peace treaty has been signed with full normalization of relations.

In this hypothetical scenario, you would end up with the following statistics:

- *Palestine: A Muslim/ Arab state with a 14% Jewish population &*

- *Israel: A Jewish state with a 22% Arab/Muslim population.*

The Palestinian population will continue to grow more rapidly than the Israeli population (33 percent higher than Israel's current rate of population growth) because of higher fertility rates among Palestinian women, 4.5 children per woman.

Whereas the Israeli population is expected to increase by about 40 percent by 2035, the Palestinian population is projected to increase by over 60 percent. If the West Bank were to be incorporated into Israel, the Jewish proportion overall would be a declining majority, 57 percent in 2014 to 53 percent in 2035 to under 49% by 2050.

History and Psychology

We can see from the above that notwithstanding the rapid increase in settlement activity in the West Bank, globally speaking, the net beneficiary of present day demographics would in the long run still be the Palestinians.

Israeli is opposed to the return the West Bank to the Palestinians for several reasons.

The first, which is often glossed over and rarely admitted is the "real estate" factor. (Israel proper is only 8,367 square miles which fits into Texas 31 times and into California 18 times!)

The second often quoted reason is the religious historical connection based on the biblical assertion that God promised the land of Judea and Samaria to the patriarch Abraham. This is the reason given by the Israeli right wing to hold on to the West Bank.

The third and the most important reason is the matter of security. Israel asserts that unilaterally returning the West Bank to the Palestinians would seriously endanger its own security. It cites the example of Gaza which it unilaterally returned to the Palestinians in 1994 without a peace treaty resulting in a takeover of the strip by the terrorist organization Hamas, whose leader is a protégé of the state of Qatar. Hamas then went on to use the country as a launching pad for missiles, terrorist raids and suicide bombers against Israeli citizens.

The question of vulnerability of Israel is an understandable concern of survival. The breach of this psychological barrier is a prerequisite to any future Israeli concession to the Palestinians. Since the Gaza debacle the Israelis are not prepared to take any further risks. This "freeing of the psyche" will inevitably remove all obstacles in the way of setting up a framework of a mutually recognized two state solution resulting in the cessation of territory acquisition by Israel.

The Palestinian leadership, on the other hand, uses the settlements as the main reason for their refusal to enter negotiations with Israel It is worth bearing in mind that ultimately the Palestinian leadership is not master of its own destiny. The financiers and supporters of Hamas and other extremist organizations in the region, mostly Qatar & Saudi Arabia (the Godfathers of Terror and Extremism) and other Gulf states have no interest in peace between the Palestinians and the Israelis. They are the puppet masters of the invisible game of control. They are content with the status quo. Peace in the region will unleash many problems for these states including possibly the questioning of their very own legitimacy. That is why Qatar's propaganda mouthpiece Aljazeera Arabic never ceases to fan the flames of conflict and hatred between Palestinians and Israelis.

The creeping colonization of the West bank by Israel will continue if there is no peace between the parties. To the Israelis this as a form of demographic defence. There is very little that anyone can do to stop this other than the usual protestations and the occasional UN resolution. Add to this, the new US administration of Donald Trump appears to be more responsive and sympathetic to Israeli demands.

Hope or Despair?

As neither the Palestinians nor the Israelis are willing or able to move forward by themselves, there is only one way to break this deadlock: A Sadat-style unconditional recognition of the State of Israel by all Arab/Islamic states. This will remove the major Israeli objection to returning the West bank to the Palestinians. Only such a momentous act will force the Palestinian leadership to settle with the Israelis and remove the underlying anxiety of the Israelis which is at the root of all their dealings with the Arabs. As one eminent Israeli professor put it to me recently "We have learnt our lessons; we will not accept anything less".

Now that most Arab states particularly the influential Gulf states share a common enemy with Israel namely Iran the collective recognition of Israel should, in theory, be less problematic. Acceptance of Israel's right to exit will render the issue of settlements peripherical and resolvable and who knows, in an economically integrated Palestine-Israel, the West Bankers might even find it advantageous to invite the settlers to stay on in the West Bank!

Is this a realistic scenario? Is a full Arab recognition of Israel likely to happen anytime soon?

As we are now in the midst of a dark age of Islamic Salafism brought about by these very same Arab states, notably Qatar and Saudi Arabia, who happen to be the sponsors and financiers of the major Sunni/Salafist terrorist organizations in the region, the foreseeable outlook appears gloomy. The very legitimacy of the Saudi royal family will be in great danger if they inflame the anti -Semite, anti-Western Wahhabi sect that underwrites this ruling dynasty's political legitimacy.

Consequently, more settlements will be built resulting in more futile complaints by the Palestinians. The status quo will prevail.

The Price of Silence

Many observers of the Middle East wonder why the financiers of terrorists, mainly in Qatar & Saudi Arabia are rarely mentioned. Where are the western demands for Qatar, and Saudi Arabia to stop funding international terrorism or being complicit in the rise of jihadi groups?

ISIS has a budget of over 2 billion pounds' courtesy of these countries. Qatar plays host not only to Taliban representatives but also to the master terrorist Khaled Mechaal, the leader of Hamas who is enjoying the largess of his Qatari hosts while his people in Gaza are being sacrificed at the altar of the group's reckless and self-serving adventurism.

Qatar's propaganda, via its mouthpiece of Al-Jazeera Arabic in support of the discredited Muslim brotherhood in Egypt and in its subtle -and often not so subtle- campaigns to brainwash the Arab masses to sympathize with extremist Sunni Muslim groups everywhere, is relentless.

And lest we forget, this is the country that has corruptly bought off FIFA members to host the world cup in 2022 and to whom we will be entrusting the safety and security of our athletes.

Qatar is also considered by many to be a friend of the west with investments in football clubs, department stores, hotels etc. In Britain "Qatar owns lucrative chunks of the county such as the Shard, a big portion of Sainsbury's and a slice of the London Stock Exchange."

And paradoxically Qatar is host to the biggest American airbase in the Middle East!

Similarly, Saudi Arabia's contribution to worldwide terror rarely gets a mention even though the country occupies an honorary position among the world's terrorist states. Western leaders have perfected the art of sycophancy in dealing with this oil rich "ally". Saudi Arabia has become an expert in buying everyone's silence with its bottomless supply of petrodollars. As an example Germany's development minister, Gerd Mueller, was recently slapped down by his government after pointing the finger at Qatar for funding the Islamic State (ISIS /DAESH).

In a rare moment of public outrage Hilary Clinton recently stated that *"It is long past time for the Saudis, Qataris and Kuwaitis and others in the region to stop their citizens from funding extremist organisations"*. Notice the use of the less direct attack on those countries by attributing the financing of terror not to the governments themselves but to "their citizens"!! This statement blatantly fails to recognise the pivotal role of the nation of Saudi Arabia in supporting terrorism.

In totalitarian states like Qatar and Saudi Arabia no "powerful private individuals" within the state would be operating without the knowledge and acquiescence of the rulers. According to a secret memo signed by the then secretary of State Hillary Clinton, Qatar has the "worst record of counter-terrorism cooperation" with the US.

Let us look at some facts:

- *Saudi Arabia is the cradle and patron of Wahhabism, the seventh century Salafist, literalist Sharia -based theology by which the country is governed.*

- *More than 2500 people have been publicly beheaded in the Kingdom over the last two decades. Go to any Saudi city on Friday after midday prayer and you will witness the grisly spectacle of beheading being theatrically choreographed as "a warning to others" It is worth pointing out that beheading, the preferred method of execution at the time of the prophet, was first re-introduced in the Kingdom of Saudi Arabia long before the Islamic State came into existence. Saudi Arabia is in fact the first contemporary Islamic State par excellence.*

- *At great expense and with total impunity Saudi Arabia caries out an extensive program of mosque building throughout the world aimed at exporting their version of Islam (Wahhabism) These mosques have acquired a reputation of being centres of extremism where young and gullible individuals are groomed and recruited by fundamentalist imams into jihadi movements. The mosques have also become collection centres for "charities" which funnel money to dubious organizations throughout Arabia and the Islamic world. And lest we forget Saudi Arabia is the country which strictly forbids those who belong to other religions to set foot in their sacred cities nor to build churches or synagogues in the Kingdom.*

- *Fifteen of the Nineteen terrorists who attacked the Twin Towers in New York in September 2001 were Saudis. Instead of attacking and occupying the guilty party Saudi Arabia (with whom the US had and continue to have massive financial and business interests), President George W Bush directed his country's fury on a soft target Iraq with many disastrous consequences.*

- *On September 23, 2016, President Barack Obama vetoed the Justice Against Sponsors of Terrorism Act which would have given the 9/11 victims' families the right to sue in US*

In conclusion those countries know that their wealth buys them the silence of the terrorist organizations they support. Their unwritten concordat with the terrorists as professor Paul Stevens of Chatham House succinctly puts it is "don't piss inside my tent, piss outside".

Their money also buys them the silence of Western governments who have learnt to look the other way and whose lips shall remain sealed as long as the petrodollars keep pouring in.

The world is now waking up to the astronomical price of silence: terror.

Puritans and Sophisticates

Puritans

Islamist seventh century man strikes again. This time his target was a Jordanian Christian/atheist Cartoonist, Nahed Hattar, who was assassinated for the crime of sharing Allah cartoon in a local paper.

Seventh century man roams the world in the twenty first century, oblivious of the passing of time. A throwback, a mutation from a distant past he is to be found everywhere: in Europe, in the Americas and in many other corners of the globe.

His journey started in his "sacred" homeland in Arabia. His sublime role model is the infallible prophet on whom he mirrors his everyday life and actions. He is in fact Abd u Allah (the slave of Allah). That is why quite often he and those of his ilk have names that start with the letters abd (slave) followed by one of the ninety-nine names of Allah. His relationship with the Allah (and his prophet) is that of Master and Servant.

Unwavering in his convictions he is essentially a puritan, a true Muslim who follows the scriptures scrupulously. Groomed from birth by said scriptures his narrative is not open to different interpretations, nuances nor doubt.

He is propelled by a subconscious inner drive to hold all his attitudes and beliefs in harmony and to avoid any cognitive dissonance. Even though he could be born in London, New York, Paris or anywhere away from his ancestral homeland, he will have built an iron clad shield around his mind to stop it from being polluted by the cultural influences of the society in which he is physically domiciled.

In most instances, he is an un-schooled simpleton, with a binary outlook on the world consisting of us - bait al Islam, the house of Islam and them -al Kuffar- the infidels who do not belong to bait al Islam.

The result of this compelling urge to maintain cognitive consistency takes a heavy toll on him and gives rise to a psychotic bi-polarism resulting in criminally irrational and manipulative behaviour.

To his mind though he is a true Muslim and not a terrorist. He is the one who executes the edicts of his master as written in the book. His murderous acts are always preceded by the declaration that Allah U Akbar (God is the greatest). In other words, as God's obedient and unquestioning servant, he is justifying to himself and to the world that the action he is about to undertake will be done in fulfilment of Allah's wishes. "Oh Master I am about to execute your commands!"

As a puritan he was groomed to believe that those who disobey the will of Allah and the prophet must be dispatched to Jahannam -the inferno where the they will burn for eternity.

Fear of Jahannam is the major reason for his actions. Seventh century man, domiciled in the twenty first century, is crippled by fear. This is why, whenever he is instructed to eliminate a kaffir, he jumps at the opportunity to achieve martyrdom. As he has learnt from birth, al shahada-martyrdom- will speedily dispatch him to Al -Janna, paradise where he will be rewarded with endless supplies of wine and women, the terrestrial pleasures he is denied (or denies himself) while in transition on earth from the present fleeting existence he is enduring, to the eternal and blissful afterlife.

Sophisticates

Seventh Century Man also roams the globe in a somewhat different re-incarnation. This version of seventh century man is far more sophisticated in his pronouncements than his fellow Puritan. A Sophisticate, he too will have lived in the West for many years if not all his life. He has mastered the art of narrative deception making his pronouncements sound conciliatory and moderate in order not alienate his Western interlocutors.

Unlike his fellow Puritan he is highly intelligent and educated in some of the top universities in the land. He has no reservation in referring to himself as a Muslim. However, he never ceases to protest that "Islam is a religion of peace" and that "terrorists are not real Muslims nor do they speak for Islam" He has perfected the art of manipulating the facts in order to back up his "moderate "narrative.

Sophisticates and Puritans have one fundamental thing in common. They both abhor change in the religious doctrine that binds them and determines their world view and their everyday life.

A Sophisticate would never be heard questioning the word of Allah as "written" in the Holy Book, nor advocating the reform of the Quran that controls his very existence. That would amount to blasphemy which is a serious crime in Islam punishable by death. (Qur'anic verses that support the many Hadith that establish the death sentence for apostates are Quran verses 2:217, 9:73-74, 88:21, 5:54, 9:66.) He is equally gripped by fear and psychological bi-polarism.

When asked by Richard Dawkins in a recent Oxford University debate - whether he believes that Mohammad flew on a winged horse to meet up with Allah in the heavens and on his way there and back alighted in Jerusalem, British born Mehdi Hassan a journalist of renown with a degree from Oxford university replied emphatically that he did *because as a Muslim I believe in everything written in the*

Quran". And for good measure he also added that he teaches his daughter the Quran including the tale of the winged horse!

"But you are an educated man of the twenty-first century!" retorted Dawkins committing his only faux pas of the evening. What in fact Dawkins should have said *"I am not surprised to hear this from you coming as it does from a seventh century man transplanted in the 21st century"*.

May be Dawkins did not realise that the Sophisticate is as literalist in his interpretation of the Muslim scriptures as his fellow puritans.

The only difference between the Sophisticates and the Puritans is that, for a variety of reasons, Sophisticates shy away from the use of physical violence.

The Future

Reza Aslan the Iranian American historian of religion wrongly believes that Islam's Reformation has been going on for the last one hundred years. He cites as examples the numerous convulsions, uprisings and terrorist -led organizations that have swept the region throughout the last century.

None of those was meant to reform Islam; they were uprisings against foreigners (colonialists),

Kuffar (infidels), or local corrupt rulers. Not one of those movements ever called for the reform of the religion itself upon which their entire political and social edifice is constructed. Rather, they all emphasised that "هوالحل الاسلام" Islam is the solution.

Islamic reform beginning with the reformation of the Quran itself has not started yet; who would have dared start it when all Muslims believe that the Quran is "the word of Allah which cannot be altered". Also, in the absence of a higher Islamic authority- a church- that speaks for Islam (everyone and no one speaks for Islam today) who in the Muslim world would dare be the bearer of the first torch of radical Islamic reform?

In the end however reason, science and technology will prevail. Cultures based on ancient myths and beliefs will ultimately be swept away. In the words of Charles Darwin 1809 "it is not the strongest of the species that survives, nor the most intelligent, but the one most responsive to change".

The Islamic world is decades if not centuries away from making this paradigm shift.

In its infancy, Islam was spread by means of "ghazo" (raids) where the nascent "religion" was forced upon the neighbouring communities by force of arms. From its base in the Hejaz the armies of Islam then went on to occupy the entire Arabian Peninsula and continued its march into Asia and

North Africa and southern Europe imposing by force of arms its new ideology. What Islam brought was not just a religion (a spiritual relationship between Man and God) but a body politic aimed at regulating the totality of every aspect of Man's daily life. It declared itself as both a religion and a state in one. Its reference was the Quran –the red line no one has ever been permitted to cross.

Those who chose not to convert to Islam were subjected to –al jizya, a punitive tax, the burden of which many could not bear and were subsequently forced to convert to Islam. ISIS applies this tax on all the non-Muslims currently under its rule in Syria and Iraq.

The occupied people were not embraced into the religion through proselytising or induction; nor were they given the choice to take the new religion or leave it. Those who chose not to give up their religion (mostly Christians and Jews) were assigned the distinctive label of "ahl al-thimma" (the people of conscience/ the book) by which they were identified throughout Islamic history. Their survival depended on their strict compliance with the laws and restrictions imposed upon them by the Muslim victors who in return bestowed upon them "himaya" a label which meant protection- albeit conditional- but which essentially implied subjugation as second class citizens.

Islamic historians have distorted these facts. AL-ghazo (raiding) is referred to with the benign designation of al-fath (liberation) and never with the correct description: occupation. The extreme violence used in al fath was justified in the same way as violence against the "infidels" is justified today by Salafist Islamic terror groups such as ISIS.

The obfuscation of historical narrative in Islam is glaring. You would never read of Islamic imperialism/colonialism in Islamic history books. The Muslims did not invade and occupy Spain for five centuries, they "liberated" it to spread the word of Allah. Those who are taken in by the myth that Islam is a religion of peace would do better to acquaint themselves with Islam's use of violence as an instrument of policy throughout its history. Islam was spawned by violence, it expanded by violence, and its only means of asserting and continuing its existence is through violence and intimidation. Violence is in its genetic make-up, in its DNA. To those who dismiss this statement with the usual platitudes "generalization ""selectivity ""Islamophobia" I say: read the Quran in its Arabic original first.

Understanding the historical roots of violence in Islam is imperative in order to understand the present day convulsions sweeping the Islamic world and spilling over to other parts of the world, and to understand how Islam views non-Muslims.

The diagnosis has to start with the Quran on which the entire edifice is built. And herein lies the dilemma. Will the Quran, a text of the 6th century with striking similarity in content and tone to the Old Testament, ever be updated to a New Quran to reflect the march of time and the monumental changes in Islamic societies in the 21st century?

Highly unlikely, not only because the Quran is "the word of Allah which cannot be altered", but also because of the absence of a higher Islamic authority- a church- that speaks for Islam. In fact, everyone and no one speaks for Islam.

(By the 4th century AD, the Old Testament was deemed irrelevant to the "modern" times and was set aside in favour of a benign and less invasive version, the New Testament., thought to be more likely to appeal to the vast majority of adherents. Over the following centuries this new version was in turn assigned to the spiritual domain only).

To understand this is vital; to ignore it is suicidal political correctness.

Islam at the Crossroad of History: Sink or Swim

Muslims are at a crossroad of destiny, they face a bleak future as long as they continue to "live in the seventh century" and discuss issues framed by seventh century's ideas.

The recent rise of Islamic Salafism (a yearning to the seventh century, the early days of Muhammad and the rise of Islam) is due to a number of reasons but primarily due to state collapse which provided the fertile breeding ground for the growth of numerous extremist groups representing the two major strands in Islam, Sunnis and Shias. Both operate through their proxy creations in most countries in the region., the Sunnis via a plethora of extremist terror groups such as AL Qaeda, ISIS (aka Daesh), al-Nusra Front and others, while the Shias operate via the Lebanon-based Hizb Allah and other Shia offshoots.

The Sunni groups are nurtured and financed by Qatar, Kuwait and Saudi Arabia. According to a recent Brookings report the majority of funds transfers go via Kuwait which has become the hub for financial transfers to most extremist Sunni groups who are Inspired by the Salafist Saudi ideology of Wahhabism while the Shia's affiliates are sponsored, finance and armed by Iran. Both Iran and Saudi Arabia continue to stoke the fires of Sunni-Shia conflict to serve their own ends although the Saudi contribution is far greater than that of Iran as the Shia are a minority in the region.

THE Sunni groups are the deadliest and most dangerous of all the terror organizations. They embrace both the political extremism of Syed Al Qutb, the ideologue of neo Islamic fundamentalism in the 60s and 7os together with the ultra-conservative cultural and social tenets of Wahhabism.

The Arabs have always been tormented by the question of why they find themselves at such a disadvantage vis-a vis the rest of the world. They have struggled to understand how they could possibly compete with more developed nations.

Why have Islam Arab countries so totally failed to create democracy for their 400 million people is one of the most frequently asked questions of the twenty first century. What makes Islam Arab society susceptible to dictatorships and fanatics bent on destroying their countries and people? Are Arabs so steeped in seventh century tribal patriarchy that they only feel safe and secure under the totalitarian rule of a father figure? Or do they suffer from a vast inferiority complex viz a viz the West resulting in their reflexive rejection of all Western institutions including Western democracy? To put it differently are Islam and democracy utterly incompatible? The answer is a resounding yes.

Islam, is at the core of most of the Arabs' troubles. The faith's claim, to combine spiritual and earthly authority, with no separation of mosque and state, has stunted the development of independent political institutions. Why bother with building and questioning anything when "the Quran, the undisputed and final word of Allah has all the answers"!! Consequently, Arab countries have failed in fostering the institutional prerequisites of democracy—the give-and-take of parliamentary discourse, protection for minorities, the emancipation of women, a free press, independent courts and universities and trade unions.

In the business and economic spheres Islam's control of all activities led to the extinguishing and strangulation of all aspects of a liberal economy. The state alone is in the driving seat. To give but one example privatisation in most Arab nations is carried out for the benefits of cohorts of the ruling elites. Virtually no markets are free, barely any world-class companies developed, and entrepreneurial Arabs who wanted to excel in business or scholarship had to go to America or Europe to do so."

Muslims do not believe in free speech nor in freedom of religion. The mere talk of secularism and human rights is anathema to the Arab mind. Coupled with this is the deeply rooted irrational and self-defeating hatred of Israel, America and the West.

There has been depressingly little discussion among Muslims of what is wrong with the Islamic world to have produced evil killers such as ISIS and Al-Qaida and thousands more like them roaming the world and wreaking horror and indiscriminate murder on innocent civilians. Worse of all the same old Islamic arrogance still prevails: it's all the West's fault and it's the West who must apologise for its imperialism and for being centuries more advanced than the Arabs!

The net result of all this is civilizational decline: pluralism, education and open markets are in decline everywhere in the Islam. Arabia world Rulers' narrative consists of one message only "the need for stability and military preparedness for the coming war to destroy and eliminate the enemy, Israel. This narrative is peddled to their hapless populations as the panacea for all societies' ills. Until these glorious aims are fulfilled all the resources of the state will be deployed for the patriotic achievement of this outcome. Meantime all the ills of society are blamed not on Islam but on Israel and its patron, the "Great Satan" the USA.

The status quo will continue while the traditional crippled Arab culture of the 7th century continues to prevail. This seems likely in the foreseeable future as Muslims are not inclined to accept their own failures whether personally, nationally or culturally.

In other words, Arabs have got to accept that the cause of their failure is their own culture based on their 7th century totalitarian religion. Muslims including the few so-called moderates among them do not have a commitment to free themselves from the shackles of their religion's iron-clad grip on their lives. In the words of Ayaan Hirsi Ali "while all human beings are equal, cultures and religions are not. ... It is part of Muslim culture to oppress women and part of all tribal cultures to institutionalize patronage, nepotism and corruption" Ayaan Hirsi Ali, Nomad (2010).

Muslims are the victims of a tyrannical culture embodied in the culture's main pillar that is Islam which stifles innovation and critical thinking with the result that all Arab states suffer from a low level of scientific and technological knowhow, "knowledge deficit."

Most Muslims states are "hollow entities built on weak conceptual frameworks" around individual ruling dynasties. The state's main raison d'etre is to operate in the service of the ruling dynasties regardless of whether they are republics or monarchies. That is why Arab states have only been able to function under strong authoritarian regimes.

Knowledge in the Arab world is not up to par because their schools and universities place too great an emphasis on memorization and rote learning.

Creativity and ingenuity are lacking in the Islamic Arab world. And despite their extremely modern image, even the Gulf states import technology from around the world and the locals have no stake in production.

Modernisation has to stem from "the traditions and culture of the region". Until these traditions and culture have been updated, no start towards real modernisation will be made. Muslims are now at a historical crossroad. They face a stark choice: sink or swim.

Brexit, Trumpism & The Elephant in The Room

In 2016 the world was shaken by two seismic events: Britain's referendum to exit the European Union and America's election of Donald Trump as its next president.

Myths and super myths

Both cases were considered by some as a shift to the Right, a repudiation of the Left, a rebellion of the down trodden white proletariat victims of globalization and liberalism who did not seem to share in their nation's growing economic cake. Others explained both events in terms of identity politics, we are being overrun by aliens who are taking our jobs and homes, our jobs are being exported to Mexico, China is flooding us with cheap goods, and in the case of Brexit our laws are being hijacked by foreign bureaucrats in Brussels, we are losing our independence and identity as a nation.

The above statements are simplifications perpetrated by politicians' spin to a populace imbued with ignorance and fear. In the words of Stephen Colbert, we now live in the era of "truthiness" where political narrative with no basis in fact feels right to the average person who is desperate to believe in whatever fits his pre-existent attitudes. In this Not-So-Brave New World we inhabit, also referred to as the post-truth world, our deeply rooted views are our facts and all we seek are conclusions to support these facts and not ones to question them or disprove them.

The basic facts are now clear. Brexiters and Trumpers won the arguments by spreading false information however inconvenient or uncomfortable it was, bogus statistics and references to deep rooted nationalism.

Xenophobia and fear of the perceived invasion of aliens were the two issues common to all Brexiters and Trumpers, be they redundant industrial workers in Chicago, unemployed English Northerners, or English Seniors who have been witnessing the slow transformation of their country and look back with nostalgia to the "good old days". No one seems to have told the disaffected that we live in a rapidly changing world in which what applied yesterday does not necessarily apply today.

When dissected, the main arguments for Brexit (Control of money, Laws, borders and sovereignty) do not survive under the microscope of clinical scrutiny. Most of those concerns could have easily been resolved within the legal EU framework. In other words, Brexiters sold nationalist slogans which they knew would appeal to the peoples' most basic fears and ignorance. Give us our nation back was their motto unaware that in this globalized world, the days of nation states are fading away and will soon become a relic of the past.

There was however one glaring twist in the narrative relating to immigration. Whilst there was no "invasion of aliens" Europeans and Americans have become fearful of one strand of immigrants whom they rightly considered a danger to their peace and security. In Europe, this danger was ignored and glossed over by liberals and only clearly highlighted by extreme Right wing parties. In the UK Brexit chief advocate Nigel Farage referred to "reaching a Breaking Point" particularly regarding the 80 million Turks (the entire population of the country!) who would be eligible to come to Europe/England once their country became a member of the EU, which as things stand now is highly unlikely to happen.

This issue was bundled into one generic package under the heading of immigration/border security which included both migrants from outside the EU and workers from within EU nations who had the legal right to move freely within the Union.

The flaw in this argument is glaring. To give but one example, of the three million EU migrants living in the UK one million are Polish. They have the highest rate of individuals in employment among all ethnic groups in the country. Until Brexit raised its ugly head there were few issues of assimilation or integration with Poles and other East European citizens. East European immigrants do not owe loyalty to a higher authority. Also, Brexit advocates did not point out to their prospective voters that migrants are a net benefit to the growing economies of Europe in a continent of falling birth rate (1.8 per woman in the UK and much lower in most other EU nations).

EU migrants living in the UK became the unforeseen casualty of a misleading narrative by self-serving politicians who did not dare nor wished, due to Political Correctness to call a spade a spade.

Whilst there is a case for stating that mass immigration, regardless of the country of origin, has placed a heavy burden on schools, hospitals and the welfare state, which must be addressed, leaving the EU is not the answer and will not by itself address these legitimate concerns.

This brings us to the elephant in the room. Ultimately the reason why a majority voted for Brexit and for Trump can be summed up in one word, Islam or to put it more accurately the fear of the creeping islamisation of Europe. In earlier times when there was no perceived Islamic terrorism few people paid much attention to Islam as a religion. However, recent terrorist attacks in Europe as well as the arrival of over a million mostly Muslim refugees in early

2016 have stirred fear in the hearts of Europeans and focused their attention on the continent's Muslim population.

- *Germany: 5,760,000*

- *France: 4,910,000*

- *United Kingdom: 3,160,000*

- *Italy: 2.420.000*

- *Bulgaria: 1,320,000*

- *Netherlands: 1,200,000*

- *Spain: 1,000,000*

- *Belgium: 930,000*

Interest in Islam itself peaked and a lot of research and analysis of the religion is taking place. What is Islam? Is it a religion or an ideology? "Why do Muslims hate us" have become common questions asked by ordinary citizens when discussing recent events. And as Muslims clearly do hate us, why then do they keep coming to live amongst us?

Before the recent spate of terrorist attacks, calls for restrictions on Islamic immigration were few and far between and went unheeded because they came mostly from fringe right wing parties. By 2016 however every citizen in Europe knows who Islamic

State, Boko Haram, Al Qaeda, Taliban and many others are and that these organizations are responsible for all terrorism in Europe and almost everywhere else in the world. When Marie Le Pen leader of the National Front in France warned against Islamic terror, she was accused of being a racist, and an "Islamophobe" Her views on this matter and probably only on this matter are now accepted by a considerable majority of French citizens. In most EU nations, what was once considered fringe is now becoming mainstream.

After the referendum in the UK and the victory of Trumpism in the US, European centrist politicians began to wake up to this ticking bomb in the body politic of their nations. Francois Holland, the socialist President of France was reported to have confided to two Le Monde journalists recently that "France has a problem with Islam" and that "there are too many Muslim immigrants in the country". These remarks were made in private but not repeated in public. Holland's PM at the time Manuel Valls, also warned that the EU project will fall apart if the concerns of the citizens on Islamic immigration are not addressed.

Many political observers believe that now is the time for Europe's centrist political leaders to call for a complete halt on Islamic immigration. It is also time for leftists and liberals to rid themselves of their delusion that Islam is a religion of peace.

Islam of today is the very same Islam of the seventh century. Hatred and non-acceptance of others is part and parcel of the religion. Any reader of the Hadiths and of the Quran in Arabic will find numerous suras advocating violence against non-Muslims. This is where the terrorists seek justification and solace for their violence.

Unreformed seventh century Islam, in practice today, will continue to spawn terror groups who will find ample justifications for their actions in the Islamic scriptures. In other words, they will consider their terror to be no more than the fulfilment of Allah's commands.

Most citizens of Europe are now aware of this fact and see no immediate alternative other than the total ban on Islamic immigration until the seventh century scriptures on which the Islamic edifice is constructed are updated and humanised to conform to twenty first century morality and internationally accepted values.

Failing this, the alternative will inevitably be a steady drift to the bosom of extreme nationalist parties who appear to be the only parties to echo the inner fears of ordinary citizens. This alternative is catastrophic to the future stability of the continent and invokes memories of 1933. And with every terrorist attack this nightmare scenario will loom closer.

PART 2
Previous Writings

Nation Building in Islam

(First published as Dr Nimier's Phd Thesis,
May 1977, SOAS – University of London)

I don't think Donald Trump has read my book on Nation Building. Although I do not see eye to eye with everything Mr Trump says, his assertion that America- and the West - should not be involved in Nation Building in the Middle East is 100 % correct.

No leader in Islam's history has ever succeeded in establishing a "nation" in its contemporary meaning.

In fact, the raison d'etre of all Muslim states that came into existence after the first world war was to promote the aggrandizement and ambitions of the individual rulers and their families be they kings, emirs, or soldier of fortunes who usurped power through coup d'états.

In case Mr. Trump has not read the book and to save him precious time, here is its overall perspective (pp 257- 259).

Nation building in the Arab world has always been a contradiction in terms. In the Middle East, a mosaic of heterogeneous populations, loyalty was never seriously channelled towards a common allegiance to the nation. (Kemal Ataturk's experiment in Turkey was the exception, but his Islamist- minded followers, in power today, are working hard to return to the status quo ante by surreptitiously doing all in their power to re-Islamize the state).

Allegiance in all Arab and Islamic states continues to lie in the family, the sect, the tribe and above all in the Sharia as it is interpreted by those in "your group" It follows therefore that allegiance to the higher ideal of a nation was never attempted as it would have inevitably resulted in challenging the political legitimacy of the ruler which came directly from Allah.

Nationhood in its secular meaning presupposes a separation between state and religion where the state applies one set of laws equally to all citizens regardless of their tribal, religious, ethnic, gender and sexual affiliations. This ideal is alien to the Muslim psyche as Islam considers itself to be both a Din (a religion) and a ***Dawla*** (a state) in one, and the two cannot be separated.

A cohesive nation necessarily is a democratic nation. Democracy is not to be confused with rituals such as periodic voting at elections, (the outcome of all elections in the so called Arab Spring states has resulted in the replacement of one dictatorship, that of the ***Rais,*** -the leader- with another, that of the Muslim fundamentalist parties). Syria, in the throes of a destructive civil war, appears to be the next candidate to join the Islamic fundamentalist camp.

True democracy is the end result of a lengthy historical process culminating in the emergence of viable institutions, an independent judiciary, a free press, a neutral civil service, emancipation and protection of minorities, freedom of all religions and most importantly freedom from religion, and the unconditional respect for the rule of law. As professor Vernon Bogdanor of King's College London has put it recently "For democracy to survive, power needs to lie not with the people, nor with the legislature but with the constitution."

To all Muslims of the fundamentalist and literalist schools (well over half of the total populations) their undisputed constitution already exists; it is the Quran which in their view addresses and regulates all aspects of their life and as such there is no need to update it.

By the 4th century AD, the "constitution" of the early Judeo-Christian era, the Old Testament was deemed irrelevant to the "modern" times and was set aside in favour of a benign and less invasive version, the New Testament., thought to be more likely to appeal to the vast majority of adherents. Over the following centuries this new version was in turn assigned to the spiritual domain only.

Will the Quran, a text of the 6th century with striking similarity in content and tone to the Old Testament, ever be updated to a New Quran to reflect the march of time and the monumental changes in

Islamic societies in the 21st century? Highly unlikely, not only because the Quran is "the word of Allah which cannot be altered", but also because of the absence of a higher Islamic authority- a church- that speaks for Islam. In fact, everyone and no one speaks for Islam.

Also, to those same Muslims the debate on nation building is irrelevant as in their view, the nation of Islam already exists. It is the *Umma* (AL UMMA AL-ISLAMIYA) and all that is required to resuscitate it into existence is to reunite its dispersed components under a Caliph and subject to the laws of Sharia. This is the rallying cry of ISIS.

Since its 6th century the West on the other hand has produced a Magna Carta, undergone a Renaissance, a Reformation, a Scientific Revolution, an Enlightenment, and a number of popular uprisings and upheavals leading to the emancipation of all its citizens and their subsequent participation in nation building.

The mind set of Islamists, literalists and their sympathisers is rooted in the sixth century. Democracy starts with the deliverance of the individual and its foundation lies in the family, the building bloc of the nation. Here the West has succeeded in vanquishing the scourge of patriarchy and the medieval culture of machismo and established equality between men and women, a far cry from today's reality in the Islamic world where the culture of AAR & EIB (shame) SHARAF (honour as related to females' sexual conduct) and HARAM (as forbidden by Allah), reigns supreme.

The Middle East is centuries away from this ideal. Armed with the West's blueprint, can the Islamic world leapfrog a lengthy historical process and achieve in a few decades what the West took centuries to accomplish. All indications point to the contrary.

The region, in its current Islamic year of 1434 AH Hijri, is on the eve of the very same convulsions and seismic changes that began to sweep the West in and before the same year of 1434 AD."

Islamic Fundamentalism – Is There a Solution?

(first published, Los Angeles, California
13th September 1993)

The recent World Trade Centre bombing in New York and the numerous attacks on other "soft targets" in Cairo and elsewhere resulting in the death of scores of innocent people have highlighted the danger of fanatic Muslim Fundamentalists. Observers of the phenomenon of religious fanaticism despair of the unpredictability of the Islamic militants and of their indiscriminate violence. Fundamentalism is often mistakenly referred to as a by-product of economic dislocation and unfair distribution of resources. While sustained economic development and enlightened government policies as in Indonesia and Malaysia will undoubtedly keep the fundamentalists at bay for a while, they will not, by themselves, offer a long term and lasting solution to the problem.

The response of most regimes in the Middle East to the violence of the fundamentalists has fallen into one of the following patterns:

- *The wholesale and indiscriminate slaughter of thousands of Islamists as was the case in Syria a few years ago when President Assad's army killed twenty-five thousand people in the city of Hama.*

- *The containment of the fundamentalists usually on an ad-hoc and eclectic basis. This has always reflected the government's own*

*inherent indecisiveness and of their fear of
alienating the bulk of their own population.*

In Egypt, for example, when members of the
"Jama's *Islamiya*" were killing Christian Copts
(Egypt's indigenous inhabitants who pre-date the
Muslims), the government's initial response was to
make as little fuss as possible. It is only since the
terrorists started targeting foreign tourists that the
government has become more decisive in dealing
with them.

In Jordan, too, not much was said or done when
members of the "Ikhwan" and the even more fanatical
"Hizb Al-Tahrir" went on a rampage, burning
Christian owned businesses in the cities of Amman
and Zarqa. When two prominent Islamist MP's were
caught, in flagrante delicto, planting explosives
provided to them courtesy of the Ayatollahs of
Teheran, their death sentences were quickly
commuted by a king's "amnesty" and they were
released from prison after barely few weeks of
detention. "The signal the government is sending to
the fundamentalists by this action is that they can
literally get away with murder" confided in me
recently a prominent Jordanian businessman who has
had one of his factories burnt down.

In Lebanon, the medieval Shiite Hezbollah reigns
supreme in the southern part of the country, heavily

armed by the Iranians. The recent devastating invasion by Israel is only one of a series of retaliatory strikes with civilian population of the country paying the heavy price for the unchallenged presence amongst them of their unwelcome "protectors".

A different way of responding to this problem has been that of the Gulf states, the "holier than thou" approach typical of states like Saudi Arabia who is constantly trying to "out-Muslim" the fundamentalists. Saudi Arabia, in fact, claims to derive its very own political legitimacy from Islam. Most Middle East analysts, however, seem to agree that Saudi Arabia is more rigid and repressive in its application of Islamic law than Iran, as it does not recognize any concepts of civil rights and civil liberties.

Sudan also has now openly adopted this approach to Islam and, in its fundamentalist zeal, has become a major exporter of arms and terror to various groups throughout the world. The Junta of General Bahir was recently implicated in the attack on the World Trade centre in New York.

None of these measures have yielded any significant long term results in combating the terror of the fundamentalists because they failed to deal, in a draconian manner with the root cause of the problem.

The roots of the problem of the Islamic fundamentalism lie in the origin of Islam itself. Islam, unlike Christianity, was born in a civic vacuum, i.e., in a tribal society where no laws existed to regulate human behaviour and endeavour. By necessity, therefore, Islam was obliged to define not only the individual's relationship with God, but also to provide a set of rules and regulations to define one's conduct in everyday life and in dealings with the newly emerging Islamic state.

These rules served Arabian man (and I use the word "man" by choice) very well in the heyday of the Islamic nation and throughout its subsequent burst of rapid expansion. And if religion is society transfigured, Islam was certainly the tribal society par excellence. It was, in other words, the Bedouin mind projected into the realm of religion.

Although times have changed since (there are very few Bedouin left!), and societies all over the world have marched into the twenty first century, Islam has remained transfixed in its roots, carrying within it the answers to all the social, economic and political ills and woes of the universe.

What then is the long-term solution to this seemingly intractable problem?

Most analysts seem to agree that the answer must surely lie in the establishment of a genuine secular democracy that would guarantee the rights of all citizens, ethnic, racial, and religious minorities. There are a few sceptics however who, for a variety of reasons, still argue that the Arabs are "not yet ready" for democratic rule. These are also joined by a variety of Arab potentates such as King Fahd of Saudi Arabia who, with a vested interest in the status quo, has publicly stated that "democracy Is not a suitable system for our religion". What the king also omitted to mention was that democracy has never actually existed in any Muslim community throughout history except for modern Turkey.

But whilst everyone agrees on the goal of democracy, with its built-in checks and balances, very few seem to know whether that goal is at all attainable and, if it is, how best to reach it... Many Western governments sought to encourage "free and fair elections" mostly in the hope of justifying to their electorate their continued support of autocratic regimes that serve Western interests in the region. What they failed to understand, however, was that real democracy could not be built on the shallow and shifting sands of the Middle East, without the inevitable risk of collapse. "Free elections" as were attempted in Algeria (only to be abandoned dramatically half way through the process), the Yemen, and soon in Jordan are no more than cosmetic attempts at siphoning off peoples' clamour for participation in the political process. At the same time, they bestow legitimacy on the ruling oligarchies without the risk and pain inherent in building the prerequisite foundations on which to erect a lasting political edifice.

Truly free elections at this juncture, based on the principle of "one man, one vote", would only result in the hijacking of the state by the fundamentalist majority just as the National Socialists did in Germany in the 1930's. It will certainly be a case of one man one vote, ONE time which will usher in a new dark age of fundamentalist rule which in turn will proceed to extinguish democracy in the name of Islam. For despite their Machiavellian commitment to democracy (several religious parties pay lip-service to the process of free elections), Islamists have no genuine regard for universal human rights, political tolerance and pluralism.

Another important pointer to this inevitable conclusion lies in the unique nature of Islam itself, being that it is both a religion and a state in one. Islamic law thus is not legislated by man but divinely revealed by Allah and, as such, it is, in the words of Professor Martin Kramer in a recent "COMMENTARY" article "perfect law which is beyond reform, abrogation or alteration". Islamic law, unlike the Universal Declaration of Human Rights, restricts one's choice of religion and spouse and grants non-Muslim minorities protection rather than equal status. An Islamic state, should it ever come into existence through free elections, will inevitably end up becoming a theocracy ruled in the name of Allah by His representative on earth. In Islamic law, Allah alone governs, even though He does so through His terrestrial deputy regardless of whether he, the deputy, was appointed, elected, or even usurped power by force. He will thus be entitled to full obedience if He exercises power (or claims to exercise it) in accordance with the laws of the Koran and the Sharia. Opposition to the government will be considered disobedience of Allah and, as such, it is a crime severely punishable in Islam. Therefore, it has always been rare to find organized "loyal" opposition governments in the Arab and Muslim states. This historical fusion between religion and state has always been the perfect recipe for the perpetuation of dictatorship and the main reason democracy has never flourished in any Arab state, at any time in history.

Elections are not the immediate answer to radical change and to the modernization of the political system. The process must then begin at the grass roots with the gradual freeing of the Arabs' mind from the "Closed Circle" of this heavy historical legacy. And while the emancipation of the Arabs must ultimately be the act of the Arabs themselves, country by country, the outside world cannot, as inter-dependent as it is, shrug off all responsibility in this process. Western governments, and particularly the U.S.A. rather than continue to call for free elections, should instead be encouraging Arab states to open up their governments to wider political participation by all those groups and individuals who are seriously committed to genuine democracy, (The West missed a great opportunity soon after the defeat of Saddam Hussein when, at a stroke, they could have rid the Middle East of both an evil dictator and a dreadful feudal sheikh AND insisted on the Introduction of genuine democratic constitutions in both Kuwait and Iraq just as they did in Germany and Japan after the Second World War. Such courageous action would in due course have generated a great deal of good will and appreciation among ordinary Arabs, while at the same time spared the Iraqis many more years of Saddam's brutality). The West should use all its influence with the Arab States to free their press and to guarantee uncensored freedom of information (at present seriously lacking in most countries), and to open public debate on the role of religion in society.

No progress can be made on the road to democracy and universal human rights in the Arab World until and unless Islam's relationship to the state has been redefined on an entirely new and contemporary basis. (Arab public opinion-makers should perhaps take a good look at Thomas Jefferson's charter of religious freedom). The demise of the Soviet Union and the passing of the cold war frees the West from the necessity of "looking the other way" whenever the tyrants and the feudal sheikhs of the Middle East are in violation of their peoples' human rights.

Put differently, the first essential step towards establishing a democratic order in the Arab and Muslim states is the immediate retirement of Allah from the political domain and for the transfer of His authority to its tangible "owners", the people. This has al-ways been at the roots of Islam's inability to solve the problem of political legitimacy, orderly succession and true governments' accountability.

The time for an Arab Reformation has now arrived. Islam's two components "Bait Al-din" and "Bait Al-*Dawla*" are now due for their final separation. The former (The House of God) will undoubtedly continue to be one of the world's three important monotheistic religions and will remain an integral part of Eastern man's psyche just as Christianity is to Western man; while the latter, the (House of Caesar) awaits total demolition and re-building... And for that, the Arabs must look no further than their northern neighbour, Turkey, a Muslim country which has successfully crossed this Rubicon.

Why has secularization eluded other Muslim and Arab states? Will it require a Turkish style revolution for this to happen? It took the imagination and boldness of one man, Kamal Ataturk, to end centuries of religious hegemony and totalitarianism. Though the Turkish experiment faced several uphill struggles, it is certainly taking roots now*. The recent election of Tansu Ciller as Turkey's first democratically elected woman prime minister is indicative of the maturity of this process. And while there are many fundamentalist stirrings in Turkey, they are no more menacing to society at large than arc the likes of David Koreish and other home grown fanatics!

Has Turkey abandoned its Muslim heritage as some of its detractors would allege? Not at all. Turkey in fact found that it did not need to renounce Islam to achieve the separation of state and religion and, as such, it prides itself on being both a secular and a Muslim society just as the U.S.A. is a secular society of Judeo-Chris-tian heritage, where freedom of religion and freedom from religion are enshrined in the constitution.

Revolution Ataturk style may no longer be feasible currently. Nevertheless, a "quiet" revolution from above carried out by a dedicated, far-sighted and a truly democratic-minded and modernizing leader (e.g. General Franco, Pinochet. Salazar) is probably still the only way out of the present political morass. The new window of opportunity that will soon offer itself when peace and normal relations between the Arab states and Israel are established will act as an important catalyst for political modernization. The Levant states will be the first beneficiary of this new Middle Fast Order. Whether they grasp this opportunity or not will be the most important challenge facing their leaders on the eve of the new millennium.

Post Script November 2016

* "Kemal Ataturk's experiment in modernism, democracy and secularism was the exception, but his Islamist- minded followers, in power today, under the authoritarian leadership of Recep Tayyip Erdoğan are working hard to return the nation to the status quo ante by doing all in their power to re-Islamize the state and to accumulate power in their own hands"

Jordanian-Palestinian Relations:

Cooperation or Drift?

No two peoples in the Middle East are more intertwined and interdependent than the Palestinians and the Jordanians. A distinct Palestinian identity has existed throughout the 20th century, but while it is true that over 60 percent of the population of Jordan is of Palestinian origin, a separate "Jordanian" identity has also evolved and matured over the last 70 years. It, too, needed to express its own autonomy, distinctiveness and self-realization. That is why advocates of the principle that "Jordan is Palestine," who are mostly on the extreme right of Israeli politics, suffer from an acute form of political myopia. You simply cannot solve the problem of one people at the expense of another.

The conduct of Jordanian-Palestinian relations cannot be isolated, or reviewed on simply a bilateral basis. It is an integral component of a larger historical dynamic; namely, the Israeli-Jordanian-Palestinian triangle. For now, Israel calls all the shots, while the Palestinians and, perhaps to a lesser extent the Jordanians, find themselves reacting to their powerful neighbour.

King Abdullah I the founder of modern Jordan was one of the first Arab leaders to understand the benefits that would accrue to the Jordanians, the Palestinians and the Israelis from cooperation and peaceful coexistence. Abdullah had a vision of a "Semitic" federation based primarily on the unity of

Palestine, Transjordan - as it was then known - and "an autonomous Jewish homeland." Today, the call is out for a free-trade area, or common market, among Israel, Jordan and Palestine. Abdullah's vision was worthy of a statesman of the greatest stature. Unfortunately, his plans came to nothing, because of the familiar chorus of indignation and opposition fanned by so-called nationalist leaders who accused him of "selling Palestine to the Jews." Today's calls of opposition to his grandson King Hussein's attempts to normalize relations with Israel are an echo of those very same self-serving, short-sighted figures from the past.

Abdullah's ideas also gave rise to a similar revolt in the ranks of the right-wing Zionists, who feared that Weizmann would be forced to give up something of the national Jewish ideal. Today's opposition by the Israeli right to the Oslo accords falls in exactly the same vein.

The reunification of the Jordanians and Palestinians, in whatever form it comes, is the most historically inevitable outcome of the long process of emancipation and political evolution of both peoples. In 1972, King Hussein put forward the idea of a federated United Arab Kingdom based on the devolution of power to the two autonomous entities of Palestine and Jordan, each with its own local parliament. local government and local budgets.

Superimposed on this sub-structure, the Kingdom would have one national parliament, one currency and one national budget.

This same conclusion is part of the "cooperation scenario" between Jordan and Palestine, envisaged by the authors of a new study by Rosemary Hollis, Mustafa Hamarneh and Khalil Shakaki, Palestine-Jordan Relations: Where to? recently published by the Royal Institute of International Affairs, London. The authors argue that "cooperation is not wholly beyond the bounds of possibility because it is a logical response to outside pressures as well as mutual interests. What has been lacking is reciprocal recognition of the legitimate interests of each side in the future stability of the other." The authors should have perhaps added that what was really lacking was Palestinian trust in the Hashemite kings - both Abdullah and Hussein - who could have delivered Palestine to them and saved both peoples from a great deal of bloodshed.

The second of the four scenarios outlined in the study, known as the "drift scenario," describes what happens in the event that none of the parties is actively involved in moving the process of final settlement forward. "All the players engage in tactical manoeuvres, but none of them can impose a broad strategy... Familial, material and psychological ties which bind the two peoples will persist along with the mutual suspicions and frictions."

The premise of the "functional scenario" is that Palestinians achieve only limited. although functional, autonomy, and both they and the Jordanians are only capable of behaving in a "reactive mode." In Jordan, this would lead to a considerable rise in disruptive opposition to the normalization of ties with Israel while in Palestine Hamas and its military wing would find greater legitimacy and support among the population. This scenario will materialize if there is no progress in the peace talks due to an Israeli government paralyzed by internal divisions and power-plays and by an American administration incapable, or unwilling. to put pressure on Israel.

If Jordan and Palestine, on the other hand. were to deliberately choose to take divergent paths. the "separation scenario" will arise. Consequently, "the Palestinian economy would end up more heavily dependent on Israel, and the Palestinians would be more isolated in their dealings with Israel, and their chances of realizing statehood would still rest on Israeli acquiescence."

Two million Palestinians live in Jordan; 150,000 Israelis live in settlements in Palestine: over 120,000 Palestinians work in Israel, and almost I millions of them live and vote in 'Israel. Palestine need not become a Bantustan to its more powerful neighbour. Its economic survival, however, is dependent on its peacefully becoming an integral part of' the open-border triangular and free trade area comprising Israel. Jordan and Palestine. Its long-term political survival, on the other hand, is dependent on its integrating with Jordan: the cooperation scenario. Back to King Hussein perhaps?

Turkey's Armenian Genocide – Will The Kurds Be Next?

Turkey has the dubious honour of being the first nation to perpetrate a genocide against its own people in the twentieth century.

By the year 1915, Turkey had already perfected its plans for the "final solution" to liquidate (expel and massacre) the two million Armenian residents of the country. Armenia was occupied by the Ottoman Empire in the 15th century. Armenians, were viewed as "Kuffar" infidels who were considered inferior to Muslims and who in compliance with Islamic Sharia law were subject to the punitive JIZYA tax and enjoyed very few political and legal rights.

Despite these tremendous obstacles, Armenians prospered. They were better educated and more resilient than their fellow Muslim citizens. Their prosperity lead to the envy and resentment of the Turkish majority. Added to this mix, the Ottoman Empire began to crumble resulting in serious dislocation and internal strife. The despotic Sultan Abdul Hamid found the perfect scapegoat in the Armenians who were blamed for all the ills of his nation by then known as the "Sick Man of Europe".

Ordinary Armenians were turned out of their homes and sent on death marches through the Mesopotamian desert without food or water. Frequently, the marchers were stripped naked and forced to walk under the scorching sun until they dropped dead. People who stopped to rest were shot.

The process of ethnic cleansing lasted almost seven years by which time 1.5 million of Turkey's two million Armenian citizens were massacred and many thousands were forcibly deported.

Records show that during this ethnic cleansing campaign government squads also kidnapped children, converted them to Islam and gave them to Turkish families. In some places, they raped women and forced them to join Turkish "harems" or serve as slaves. Muslim families moved into the homes of deported Armenians and seized their property. Several hundred Armenian intellectuals were rounded up, arrested and later executed. *

In 1908 a group of disgruntled army officers who became known as the Young Turks deposed the Sultan and seized power. The purge of the Armenians however continued until 1922. Several killing squads or "butcher battalions" as they became known were created to carry out "the liquidation of the "Christian elements." as the Armenians were referred to. These killing squads drowned people in rivers, threw them off cliffs, crucified them and burned them alive.

The Treaty of Serves between the victorious allied powers and the vanquished ottoman Empire at the end of the First World War signed in August 1920, provided for an independent autonomous Kurdistan.

Kemal Atatürk

In 1923, Kemal Ataturk a leading figure within the Turkish army, who became known as the "father of the nation", ascended to power and proceeded to de-Islamise the state "we must join the modern world" he declared. He closed all religious courts and schools, prohibited the wearing of headscarves among public sector employees, abolished the ministry of canon law and pious foundations, lifted a ban on alcohol, adopted the Gregorian calendar in place of the Islamic calendar, made Sunday a day of rest instead of Friday, changed the Turkish alphabet from Arabic letters to Roman ones, mandated that the call to prayer be in Turkish rather than Arabic and even forbade the wearing of fez hats.

Under Ataturk's leadership in other words the role of Islam in public life shrank drastically and he eventually succeeded in establishing a secular and quasi- westernized country.

On his death in November 10, 1938, Atatürk, was replaced by his prime minister Is met Inonu, who continued Ataturk's progressive policies of modernization.

Turkey's Enlightened Era 1923-2002

Between 1923-2002 Turkey enjoyed a relatively stable democratic secular era with free elections, a multi-party system, a free press and an independent judiciary. The army assumed the role of the guardian of Ataturk's legacy. This period in modern Turkey's history is often referred to as Turkey's Enlightened Era during which the country elected its first female Prime Minister Tansu Ciller from 1993 to 1996.

In 2002 the democratic process led to the election of Recep Tayyip Erdogan of the conservative, Islamic Justice and development Party.

Deconstructing the State

President Recep Tayyip Erdogan is hard at work laying his own version of a final solution to crush the fifteen million Kurds in the country – a fifth of his own population. The Kurds have no political rights nor freedom of speech. Over the last decades over 2000 Kurdish villages have been destroyed and tens of thousands have been killed.

Human Rights Watch has reported that *The government's erosion of media freedom continued. Readiness to limit freedom of expression, restrictive approach to freedom of assembly, and readiness to prosecute demonstrators while tolerating police violence against them, were among features most damaging to Turkey's democratic credentials... Trials continued of Kurdish political activists, journalists, students, and lawyers on widely used terrorism charges such as 'membership of an armed organization.' The evidence against them in most cases concerned nonviolent political association and protest.*

Ailing Economy -The Rise of a Dictator

The country's ailing economy over the recent years resulted as it did at the turn of the 20th century vis a vis the Armenians, in whipping up the flames of hatred and blame against the country's Kurdish minority.

Genocide by Attrition

The purge of the Kurds continues to this day. The bombardment of Kurdish soldiers fighting the terrorist organization ISIS, financed by Turkey, Qatar and Saudi Arabia and once a friend and ally of Turkey, goes on relentlessly Erdogan is determined to crush the fifteen million Kurds in Turkey – a fifth of his own population – and is being unashamedly brutal in his campaign.

The Kurds' choice, like that of the Armenians before them and that of most minorities in Islam throughout history is stark: Assimilate or Die

Hannah L S Sikma of The Sunday Times recently referred to the war against the Kurds in Eastern Turkey as Erdogan's "hidden war" which is sweeping across the region flattening entire neighbourhoods and displacing hundreds of thousands of its inhabitants.

On the political front Erdogan's agenda is clear. He wants to replace his country's system of parliamentary government with an all-powerful executive presidency. This will give him the constitutional and legal right to issue executive and legislative decrees and have veto power over parliament as well as being able to appoint ministers and judges to higher courts, in many ways echoing Hitler &the Weimar republic of 1933.

Should the world be concerned about a second genocide in Turkey against the Kurds?

Genocides come in many forms; some take place in a short span of time and others are spread out over many years. The war of attrition started by Erdogan against his Kurdish citizens, if unchecked, will inevitably lead to the elimination of a great number of Kurds and the destruction of their homeland both in southern Turkey and Northern Syria. Let us bear in mind that Genocide is defined as *"a premeditated and systematic campaign to exterminate an entire people")*.

Genocide in the 20th Century

- *Armenians in Turkey 1915-1922*
  1,500,000

- *Stalin's Forced Famine: 1932-1936*
  7,000,000

- *Rape of Nanking:*   *1937-1938*
  300,000

- *Nazi Holocaust:*   *1938-1945*
  6,000,000

- *Pol Pot in Cambodia: 1975-1979*
  2,000,000

- *Rwanda*   *1994-1995*   *800,000*

- *Bosnia-Herzegovina   1992-1995*
  200,000

History has taught us that dictators are bullies who must be resisted. Erdogan stated that he would renege on his recent agreement with the European Union and threatened to open his borders to unleash hundreds of thousands of refugees into Europe. He is also threatening to withdraw from NATO and has already established closer ties with Russia's Putin.

His bluff must be called.

Islam & Anti-Semitism

The Root of Hatred

(From the Quran: Surat al Bakara: The Cow):

[2.88] And they say: Our hearts are covered. Nay, Allah has cursed them because their unbelief; so, little it is that they believe.

[2.98] Whoever is the enemy of Allah and His angels and His apostles and Jibreel and Meekaeel, so surely Allah is the enemy of the unbelievers.

[2.121] Those to whom We have given the Book read it as it ought to be read. These believe in it; and whoever disbelieves in it, these it is that are the losers.

Why do Saudis, Pakistanis, Algerians, Iranians, Yemenis and most other Islamic countries who were neither involved in nor touched by the Israeli - Palestinian wars keep alive a hatred of Israel and the Jews far beyond any rational explanation. Why is this hatred publicly fanned and promoted among the people as an important instrument of public policy?

Why do Muslims hate not only Israel but Jews in general?

Origins

The root of this hatred goes back to the early days of the prophet Muhammad's raids *(ghazo)* outside his hometown of Mecca to spread his new ideology, Islam. Muhammad's aim was to forcibly convert all the tribes of Arabia into his new *risala* (message) To do so he recruited an army of 7.000 men including approximately 300 horses from his Meccans and other smaller tribes who had agreed to convert to the new ideology. (W M Watt).

The Jewish tribes of Arabia, however, wanting to remain loyal to their religion and heritage chose not to join Muhammad in his new army. Muhammad reacted angrily to this rejection and to set an example to the other tribes, he expelled two minor tribes of Jews from their habitat in the Arabian Peninsula, the Qaynuqa tribe in AD 624 and the Nadir tribe in AD 625. Muhammad called on his followers to wage war on them, besieging them in their strongholds and set about destroying their palm trees and confiscating their tools of trade thus forcing them to abandon their land and migrate as far away from Arabia as they could.

The more influential Jewish tribe of Qurayzah also chose not to join Muhammad's army and to remain neutral, at which point the angel Gabriel conveniently appeared to Muhammad telling him that he is ordered by Allah to fight the Qurayzah Jews. The fate of the Qurayzah was now sealed and Muhammad was about to impose the ultimate penalty on the last remaining tribe of Jews in Medina (James M. Alanson).

In what became known as the battle of the Trench AD 627, Mohammad's army dug trenches around Medina to encircle the tribe. The Qurayzah Jews, sensing that their fate was sealed and hoping for a peaceful outcome, decided to surrender to Muhammad resulting in the mass extermination and enslavement of all the remaining Jews in the city even though they did not mount any resistance.

Ibn Ishaq, the authoritative early Islamic historian and Muhammad's biographer describes the killing of the Qurayzah men as follows:

Muhammad sent for them and personally struck off their heads in those trenches as they were brought out to him in batches. This went on until the Apostle (Muhammad) made an end of them. There were 600 or 700 in all, though some put the figure as high as 800 or 900. The spoils of battle, including the enslaved women and children of the tribe, were divided up among the Muslims that had participated in the siege".

Muhammad's successor the Caliph Omar decreed that Jews (and Christians) should be removed from all of Arabia. This became known as the Pact of Omar which also considered the Jews to be inferior to Muslims.

Throughout the middle Ages there have been numerous pogroms against Jews in Islamic- occupied lands. Faced with the choice of either death or conversion thousands of Jews were forced to migrate to more tolerant lands.

Throughout history while most invaders mainly wanted to occupy, Islamic invaders demanded conversion. The policy of cleansing the Islamic lands of Jews was based on Muhammad's words "let there be no two religions in Arabia". This saying of the prophet is rooted in the psyche of all Muslims. This is probably the main reason why Saudi Arabia-the guardian of Islam's sacred sites- does not allow the entry of non-Muslims to these places nor the building of churches and synagogues anywhere in the kingdom.

All prophets and founders of other religions have preached tolerance of others, advocated peaceful co-existence, and strongly shunned violence. Muhammad practiced violence throughout his career and considered war as an instrument of imposing his message. Throughout his career he did not shy from using bloodshed against Jews and Christians.

The armies of Islam went on to conquer the whole of Arabia, Greater Syria, North Africa, Spain and a considerable chunk of Southern Europe. Under the rule of Islam, Jews were assigned the distinctive label of "ahl *al-thimma*" (the people of conscience/ the book) by which they were identified throughout

Islamic history. Their survival depended on their strict compliance with the laws and restrictions imposed upon them by the Muslim victors who in return bestowed upon them *"himaya"* a label which meant protection- albeit conditional- but which essentially implied subjugation as inferior second class citizens.

The establishment of the State of Israel in 1948 brought to the surface the full weight of the Islamic pent-up hatred against the Jews. Most the 800.000 Jews remaining in Arab lands were expelled en masse moving to Israel, Europe and the USA.

Anti-Semitism (anti-Jewishness to be more precise) is not, as it is often explained by Islamic apologists, a territorial /political sentiment. It is a deeply rooted religious antipathy that goes back to the days of the prophet and early Islam. This blind hatred can only be extinguished when the Islamic scriptures have been reformed and a new more benevolent and all-embracing New Quran has come into existence.

References to Jews in the Koran

The Koran is divided into 114 chapters called suras. The following are translations of passages found in these suras that are related to Jews.

The Cow

*[2.40] O children of Israel! call to mind My favour
which I bestowed on you and be faithful to (your)
covenant with Me, I will fulfil (My) covenant with
you; and of Me, Me alone, should you be afraid.*

*[2.47] O children of Israel! call to mind My favour
which I bestowed on you and that I made you excel
the nations.*

*[2.62] Surely those who believe, and those who
are Jews, and the Christians, and the Sabians,
whoever believes in Allah and the Last day and does
good, they shall have their reward from their Lord,
and there is no fear for them, nor shall they grieve.*

*[2.83] And when We made a covenant with the
children of Israel: You shall not serve any but Allah
and (you shall do) good to (your) parents, and to the
near of kin and to the orphans and the needy, and you
shall speak to men good words and keep up prayer
and pay the poor-rate. Then you turned back except a
few of you and (now too) you turn aside.*

*[2.88] And they say: Our hearts are covered. Nay,
Allah has cursed them on account of their unbelief;
so little it is that they believe.*

*[2.98] Whoever is the enemy of Allah and His
angels and His apostles and Jibreel and Meekaeel, so
surely Allah is the enemy of the unbelievers.*

[2.111] And they say: None shall enter the garden (or paradise) except he who is a Jew or a Christian. These are their vain desires. Say: Bring your proof if you are truthful.

[2.113] And the Jews say: The Christians do not follow anything (good) and the Christians say: The Jews do not follow anything (good) while they recite the (same) Book. Even thus say those who have no knowledge, like to what they say; so Allah shall judge between them on the day of resurrection in what they differ.

[2.120] And the Jews will not be pleased with you, nor the Christians until you follow their religion. Say: Surely Allah's guidance, that is the (true) guidance. And if you follow their desires after the knowledge that has come to you, you shall have no guardian from Allah, nor any helper.

[2.121] Those to whom We have given the Book read it as it ought to be read. These believe in it; and whoever disbelieves in it, these it is that are the losers.

[2.122] O children of Israel, call to mind My favour which I bestowed on you and that I made you excel the nations.

[2.135] And they say: Be Jews or Christians, you will be on the right course. Say: Nay! (we follow) the

religion of Ibrahim, the Hanif, and he was not one of the polytheists.

[2.140] Nay! do you say that Ibrahim and Ismail and Yaqoob and the tribes were Jews or Christians? Say: Are you better knowing or Allah? And who is more unjust than he who conceals a testimony that he has from Allah? And Allah is not at all heedless of what you do.

[2.211] Ask the Israelites how many a clear sign have We given them; and whoever changes the favour of Allah after it has come to him, then surely Allah is severe in requiting (evil).

[2.246] Have you not considered the chiefs of the children of Israel after Musa, when they said to a prophet of theirs: Raise up for us a king, (that) we may fight in the way of Allah. He said: May it not be that you would not fight if fighting is ordained for you? They said: And what reason have we that we should not fight in the way of Allah, and we have indeed been compelled to abandon our homes and our children. But when fighting was ordained for them, they turned back, except a few of them, and Allah knows the unjust.

The Family of Imran

[3.23] Have you not considered those (Jews) who are given a portion of the Book? They are invited to

the Book of Allah that it might decide between them, then a part of them turn back and they withdraw.

[3.24] This is because they say: The fire shall not touch us but for a few days; and what they have forged deceives them in the matter of their religion.

[3.49] And (make him) an apostle to the children of Israel: That I have come to you with a sign from your Lord, that I determine for you out of dust like the form of a bird, then I breathe into it and it becomes a bird with Allah's permission and I heal the blind and the leprous, and bring the dead to life with Allah's permission and I inform you of what you should eat and what you should store in your houses; most surely there is a sign in this for you, if you are believers.

[3.67] Ibrahim was not a Jew nor a Christian but he was (an) upright (man), a Muslim, and he was not one of the polytheists.

[3.93] All food was lawful to the children of Israel except that which Israel had forbidden to himself, before the Taurat was revealed. Say: Bring then the Taurat and read it, if you are truthful.

The Women

[4.46] Of those who are Jews (there are those who) alter words from their places and say: We have heard and we disobey and: Hear, may you not be

made to hear! and: Raina, distorting (the word) with their tongues and taunting about religion; and if they had said (instead): We have heard and we obey, and hearken, and unzurna it would have been better for them and more upright; but Allah has cursed them on account of their unbelief, so they do not believe but a little.

[4.47] O you who have been given the Book! believe that which We have revealed, verifying what you have, before We alter faces then turn them on their backs, or curse them as We cursed the violators of the Sabbath, and the command of Allah shall be executed.

[4.50] See how they forge the lie against Allah, and this is sufficient as a manifest sin.

[4.160] Wherefore for the iniquity of those who are Jews did We disallow to them the good things which had been made lawful for them and for their hindering many (people) from Allah's way.

[4.161] And their taking usury though indeed they were forbidden it and their devouring the property of people falsely, and We have prepared for the unbelievers from among them a painful chastisement.

The Dinner Table

[5.12] And certainly Allah made a covenant with the children of Israel, and We raised up among them

*twelve chieftains; and Allah said: Surely I am with
you; if you keep up prayer and pay the poor-rate and
believe in My apostles and assist them and offer to
Allah a goodly gift, I will most certainly cover your
evil deeds, and I will most certainly cause you to
enter into gardens beneath which rivers flow, but
whoever disbelieves from among you after that, he
indeed shall lose the right way.*

*[5.13] But on account of their breaking their
covenant We cursed them and made their hearts
hard; they altered the words from their places and
they neglected a portion of what they were reminded
of; and you shall always discover treachery in them
excepting a few of them; so pardon them and turn
away; surely Allah loves those who do good (to
others).*

*[5.18] And the Jews and the Christians say: We
are the sons of Allah and His beloved ones. Say: Why
does He then chastise you for your faults? Nay, you
are mortals from among those whom He has created,
He forgives whom He pleases and chastises whom He
pleases; and Allah's is the kingdom of the heavens
and the earth and what is between them, and to Him
is the eventual coming.*

*[5.32] For this reason did We prescribe to the
children of Israel that whoever slays a soul, unless it
be for manslaughter or for mischief in the land, it is*

as though he slew all men; and whoever keeps it alive, it is as though he kept alive all men; and certainly Our apostles came to them with clear arguments, but even after that many of them certainly act extravagantly in the land.

[5.33] The punishment of those who wage war against Allah and His apostle and strive to make mischief in the land is only this, that they should be murdered or crucified or their hands and their feet should be cut off on opposite sides or they should be imprisoned; this shall be as a disgrace for them in this world, and in the hereafter they shall have a grievous chastisement.

[5.41] O Apostle! let not those grieve you who strive together in hastening to unbelief from among those who say with their mouths: We believe, and their hearts do not believe, and from among those who are Jews; they are listeners for the sake of a lie, listeners for another people who have not come to you; they alter the words from their places, saying: If you are given this, take it, and if you are not given this, be cautious; and as for him whose temptation Allah desires, you cannot control anything for him with Allah. Those are they for whom Allah does not desire that He should purify their hearts; they shall have disgrace in this world, and they shall have a grievous chastisement in the hereafter.

[5.42] (They are) listeners of a lie, devourers of what is forbidden; therefore, if they come to you, judge between them or turn aside from them, and if you turn aside from them, they shall not harm you in any way; and if you judge, judge between them with equity; surely Allah loves those who judge equitably.

[5.43] And how do they make you a judge and they have the Taurat wherein is Allah's judgment? Yet they turn back after that, and these are not the believers.

[5.44] Surely We revealed the Taurat in which was guidance and light; with it the prophets who submitted themselves (to Allah) judged (matters) for those who were Jews, and the masters of Divine knowledge and the doctors, because they were required to guard (part) of the Book of Allah, and they were witnesses thereof; therefore fear not the people and fear Me, and do not take a small price for My communications; and whoever did not judge by what Allah revealed, those are they that are the unbelievers.

[5.51] O you who believe! do not take the Jews and the Christians for friends; they are friends of each other; and whoever amongst you takes them for a friend, then surely he is one of them; surely Allah does not guide the unjust people.

[5:57] O you who believe! do not take for guardians those who take your religion for a mockery and a joke, from among those who were given the Book before you and the unbelievers; and be careful of (your duty to) Allah if you are believers.

[5.59] Say: O followers of the Book! do you find fault with us (for aught) except that we believe in Allah and in what has been revealed to us and what was revealed before, and that most of you are transgressors?

[5.60] Say: Shall I inform you of (him who is) worse than this in retribution from Allah? (Worse is he) whom Allah has cursed and brought His wrath upon, and of whom He made apes and swine, and he who served the Shaitan; these are worse in place and more erring from the straight path.

[5.63] Why do not the learned men [rabbis] and the doctors of law prohibit them from their speaking of what is sinful and their eating of what is unlawfully acquired? Certainly evil is that which they work.

[5.64] And the Jews say: The hand of Allah is tied up! Their hands shall be shackled and they shall be cursed for what they say. Nay, both His hands are spread out, He expends as He pleases; and what has been revealed to you from your Lord will certainly make many of them increase in inordinacy and unbelief; and We have put enmity and hatred among

them till the day of resurrection; whenever they kindle a fire for war Allah puts it out, and they strive to make mischief in the land; and Allah does not love the mischief-makers.

[5.69] Surely those who believe and those who are Jews and the Sabians and the Christians whoever believes in Allah and the last day and does good- they shall have no fear nor shall they grieve.

[5.70] Certainly We made a covenant with the children of Israel and We sent to them apostles; whenever there came to them an apostle with what that their souls did not desire, some (of them) did they call liars and some they slew.

[5.72] Certainly they disbelieve who say: Surely Allah, He is the Messiah, son of Marium; and the Messiah said: O Children of Israel! serve Allah, my Lord and your Lord. Surely whoever associates (others) with Allah, then Allah has forbidden to him the garden, and his abode is the fire; and there shall be no helpers for the unjust.

[5.73] Certainly they disbelieve who say: Surely Allah is the third (person) of the three; and there is no god but the one God, and if they desist not from what they say, a painful chastisement shall befall those among them who disbelieve.

[5.78] Those who disbelieved from among the children of Israel were cursed by the tongue of Dawood and Isa, son of Marium; this was because they disobeyed and used to exceed the limit.

[5.79] They used not to forbid each other the hateful things (which) they did; certainly evil was that which they did.

[5.80] You will see many of them befriending those who disbelieve; certainly evil is that which their souls have sent before for them, that Allah became displeased with them and in chastisement shall they abide.

[5.81] And had they believed in Allah and the prophet and what was revealed to him, they would not have taken them for friends but! most of them are transgressors.

[5.82] Certainly you will find the most violent of people in enmity for those who believe (to be) the Jews and those who are polytheists, and you will certainly find the nearest in friendship to those who believe (to be) those who say: We are Christians; this is because there are priests and monks among them and because they do not behave proudly.

[5.86] And (as for) those who disbelieve and reject Our communications, these are the companions of the flame.

[5.110] When Allah will say: O Isa son of Marium! Remember My favor on you and on your mother, when I strengthened you I with the holy Spirit, you spoke to the people in the cradle and I when of old age, and when I taught you the Book and the wisdom and the Taurat and the Injeel; and when you determined out of clay a thing like the form of a bird by My permission, then you breathed into it and it became a bird by My permission, and you healed the blind and the leprous by My permission; and when you brought forth the dead by My permission; and when I withheld the children of Israel from you when you came to them with clear arguments, but those who disbelieved among them said: This is nothing but clear enchantment.

The Cattle

[6.146] And to those who were Jews We made unlawful every animal having claws, and of oxen and sheep We made unlawful to them the fat of both, except such as was on their backs or the entrails or what was mixed with bones: this was a punishment We gave them on account of their rebellion, and We are surely Truthful.

The Elevated Places

[7.105] (I am) worthy of not saying anything about Allah except the truth: I have come to you

indeed with clear proof from your Lord, therefore send with me the children of Israel.

[7.134] And when the plague fell upon them, they said: O Musa! pray for us to your Lord as He has promised with you, if you remove the plague from us, we will certainly believe in you and we will certainly send away with you the children of Israel.

[7.137] And We made the people who were deemed weak to inherit the eastern lands and the western ones which We had blessed; and the good word of your Lord was fulfilled in the children of Israel because they bore up (sufferings) patiently; and We utterly destroyed what Faron and his people had wrought and what they built.

[7.138] And We made the children of Israel to pass the sea; then they came upon a people who kept to the worship of their idols. They said: O Musa! make for us a god as they have (their) gods. He said: Surely you are a people acting ignorantly:

The Immunity

[9.30] And the Jews say: Uzair is the son of Allah; and the Christians say: The Messiah is the son of Allah; these are the words of their mouths; they imitate the saying of those who disbelieved before; may Allah destroy them; how they are turned away!

[9:34] O you who believe! most surely many of the doctors of law [rabbis] and the monks eat away the property of men falsely, and turn (them) from Allah's way; and (as for) those who hoard up gold and silver and do not spend it in Allah's way, announce to them a painful chastisement....

Jonah

[10.90] And We made the children of Israel to pass through the sea, then Faron and his hosts followed them for oppression and tyranny; until when drowning overtook him, he said: I believe that there is no god but He in Whom the children of Israel believe and I am of those who submit.

[10.93] And certainly We lodged the children of Israel in a goodly abode and We provided them with good things; but they did not disagree until the knowledge had come to them; surely your Lord will judge between them on the resurrection day concerning that in which they disagreed.

The Bee

[16.118] And for those who were Jews We prohibited what We have related to you already, and We did them no injustice, but they were unjust to themselves.

The Children of Israel

[17.2] And We gave Musa the Book and made it a guidance to the children of Israel, saying: Do not take a protector besides Me;

[17.4] And We had made known to the children of Israel in the Book: Most certainly you will make mischief in the land twice, and most certainly you will behave insolently with great insolence.

[17.101] And certainly We gave Musa nine clear signs; so ask the children of Israel. When he came to them, Firon said to him: Most surely I deem you, O Musa, to be a man deprived of reason.

[17.104] And We said to the Israelites after him: Dwell in the land: and when the promise of the next life shall come to pass, we will bring you both together in judgment.

Marium

[19.58] These are they on whom Allah bestowed favours, from among the prophets of the seed of Adam, and of those whom We carried with Nuh, and of the seed of Ibrahim and Israel, and of those whom We guided and chose; when the communications of the Beneficent God were recited to them, they fell down making obeisance and weeping.

Ta Ha

[20.47] So go you both to him and say: Surely we are two apostles of your Lord; therefore send the children of Israel with us and do not torment them! Indeed, we have brought to you a communication from your Lord, and peace is on him who follows the guidance;

[20.48] Surely it has been revealed to us that the chastisement will surely come upon him who rejects and turns back.

[20.80] O children of Israel! indeed We delivered you from your enemy, and We made a covenant with you on the blessed side of the mountain, and We sent to you the manna and the quails.

[20.94] He said: O son of my mother! seize me not by my beard nor by my head; surely I was afraid lest you should say: You have caused a division among the children of Israel and not waited for my word.

The Pilgrimage

[22.17] Surely those who believe and those who are Jews and the Sabaeans and the Christians and the Magians and those who associate (others with Allah) -- surely Allah will decide between them on the day of resurrection; surely Allah is a witness over all things.

[22.40] Those who have been expelled from their homes without a just cause except that they say: Our Lord is Allah. And had there not been Allah's repelling some people by others, certainly there would have been pulled down cloisters and churches and synagogues and mosques in which Allah's name is much remembered; and surely Allah will help him who helps His cause; most surely Allah is Strong, Mighty.

The Poets

[26.17] Then send with us the children of Israel.

[26.22] And is it a favour of which you remind me that you have enslaved the children of Israel?

[26.59] Even so. And We gave them as a heritage to the children of Israel.

[26.197] Is it not a sign to them that the learned men of the Israelites know it?

The Ant

[27.76] Surely this Quran declares to the children of Israel most of what they differ in.

The Adoration

[32.23] And certainly We gave the Book to Musa, so be not in doubt concerning the receiving of it, and We made it a guide for the children of Israel.

The Believer

[40.53] And certainly We gave Musa the guidance, and We made the children of Israel inherit the Book,

Ornaments of Gold

[43.59] He was naught but a servant on whom We bestowed favour, and We made him an example for the children of Israel.

The Smoke

[44.30] And certainly We delivered the children of Israel from the abasing chastisement,

The Kneeling

[45.16] And certainly We gave the Book and the wisdom and the prophecy to the children of Israel, and We gave them of the goodly things, and We made them excel the nations.

The Sandhills

[46.10] Say: Have you considered if it is from Allah, and you disbelieve in it, and a witness from

among the children of Israel has borne witness of one like it, so he believed, while you are big with pride; surely Allah does not guide the unjust people.

The Banishment

[59.2] He it is Who caused those who disbelieved of the followers of the Book to go forth from their homes at the first banishment you did not think that they would go forth, while they were certain that their fortresses would defend them against Allah; but Allah came to them whence they did not expect, and cast terror into their hearts; they demolished their houses with their own hands and the hands of the believers; therefore, take a lesson, O you who have eyes!

[59.3] And had it not been that Allah had decreed for them the exile, He would certainly have punished them in this world, and in the hereafter they shall have chastisement of the fire.

The Ranks

[61.6] And when Isa son of Marium said: O children of Israel! surely I am the apostle of Allah to you, verifying that which is before me of the Taurat and giving the good news of an Apostle who will come after me, his name being Ahmad, but when he came to them with clear arguments they said: This is clear magic.

[61.7] And who is more unjust than he who forges a lie against Allah and he is invited to Islam, and Allah does not guide the unjust people.

[61.14] O you who believe! be helpers (in the cause) of Allah, as~ Isa son of Marium said to (his) disciples: Who are my helpers in the cause of Allah? The disciples said: We are helpers (in the cause) of Allah. So a party of the children of Israel believed and another party disbelieved; then We aided those who believed against their enemy, and they became uppermost.

The Congregation

[62.6] Say: O you who are Jews, if you think that you are the favourites of Allah to the exclusion of other people, then invoke death If you are truthful.

The Plight of Christians in Islamic Lands

A Genocide That Dares Not Speak Its Name

"In all its history, Islam has shown a warlike and conquering face; for almost a thousand years, Europe lived under its constant threat. What remains of the Christian population in Islamic countries is still subjected to perpetual discrimination with regular episodes of bloody persecution:

Giuseppe De Rosa, S.I.

Most anti-Christian persecution in the world took place at the hands of Muslims.

American scholar Raymond Ibrahim wrote that "the overwhelming majority of Christian `persecution around the world today is being committed at the hands of Muslims of all races, languages, cultures and socio-political circumstances: Muslims from among America's allies (Saudi Arabia) and its enemies (Iran); Muslims from economically rich nations (Qatar) and from poor nations (Somalia and Yemen); Muslims from 'Islamic republic' nations (Afghanistan) and from 'moderate' nations (Malaysia and Indonesia); and Muslims from nations rescued by America (Kuwait)."

Ibrahim noted that in countries that underwent "Arab Spring" uprisings, increased persecution occurred after the regimes collapsed. "Muslim persecution of Christians," Ibrahim wrote, is "part of a continuum that started nearly 14 centuries ago."

This ongoing religious persecution is forcing millions of Christians to flee their homes. Christians are disappearing from entire regions in the Middle East particularly in the land where Christianity was born, Palestine.

In other Middle East countries (Lebanon, Syria, Jordan, Iraq), there were flourishing Christian populations prior to the Islamic invasion and occupation of the region. Today there are only small Christian communities remaining.

In Africa, the situation is not much better. Most Christians in northern Nigeria have fled their homes where the Islamist terror group Boko Haram is waging a campaign of terror against Christians in the country.

In the Maghreb states, there were numerous Christian communities before the Muslim invasion. After the Arab conquest, Christianity was absorbed by the occupying Islam to such an extent that today Christianity has a presence only in Egypt represented by the Coptic church which makes up 8% percent of the Egyptian population. This number is decreasing by the year.

Christian women and girls in Muslim countries have always been particularly vulnerable due to the repression prompted by their gender and the hostility and persecution that comes from their minority

Christian faith. In Pakistan and Afghanistan women are regularly abducted and raped for minor infringements of the Islamic dress code.

The Middle East continues to be a major hub of anti-Christian persecution. David Alton the crossbench peer and campaigner on the issue, described events in Syria and Iraq as "a genocide that dares not speak its name".

In all the places where Islam imposed itself by military force Christianity practically disappeared or was reduced to tiny pockets in an endless sea of Islamic rule. Reduction of Christianity to small minorities was not only due to violent religious persecution, but to the conditions in which Christians were forced to live within the occupying Islamic state. Throughout its history, Islam has shown a disdain for the "infidels" who were given a choice: to convert to Islam, pay the dhimma (a punitive tax) be deported from Islamic lands or be eliminated or killed." (Quran, Sura 9:29).

Did Christians ever enjoy harmony and equality under Islamic rule? Was there a cultural golden age in Islamic Spain, with Muslims, Christians and Jews living in harmony as we have been made to believe through myths and uncorroborated facts?? Irrefutable evidence points to the contrary. America Castro, who coined the word convivence to describe the life of the three faiths in Spain, wrote, in his book The Structure of Spanish History: "Each of the three peoples of the peninsula saw itself forced to live for eight centuries together with the other two at the same time as it passionately desired their extermination."

The tension was only resolved in the "Reconquista" of Spain by the Christians. Spain in fact was the only territory long under an Islamic rule where Christians did not dwindle into a helpless minority. This is primarily due to the fact that Muslims did not constitute the majority of the population...

Another exaggerated myth is that of the Islamic contribution to Western civilization. No doubt some Muslim scholars in the "Golden Age" of Islamic expansion- 9th to 13th centuries- such as al-Khwarizmi made a valuable contribution to mathematics (algebra) and astronomy while others acted as conduits for translating Greek and Persian science texts. What is less known however is that most of these translations were carried out by Christians and Jews.

One such prominent translator was Patriarch Timothy I of the Church of the East who lived in Baghdad.at the height of the Abbasid Caliphate. Patriarch Timothy, who ruled his church for 43 years, translated Aristotle's Topics for the caliph al-Mahdi, in whose court he conversed with other Aristotelian philosophers on knowledge and the doctrine of God.

Cri de Coeur

The Status of Christians In today's Islamic world is no better than it has always been throughout history if not much worse. The following statistics speak volume for their unhappy plight. Each month in Islamic countries 322 Christians are killed, 214 churches and properties are destroyed and 722 forms of violence and abuse are perpetrated against them. *

The latest Islamic acts of terrorism in Europe and around the world, triggered panic among people who became aware of the danger of uncontrolled Islamic immigration. Calls for a stop on immigration from Islamic nations can be heard everywhere. While this is understandable and in some instances justified, the worry is that the Christian minorities in those countries who are at the forefront of Islamic persecution will fall victim to this ban and pay the heaviest price.

"Christians in Islamic countries today do not practice crucifixion, stoning or beheading of their opponents nor do they blow themselves up to kill innocent bystanders" confided a Christian colleague in a recent debate on Muslim immigration to America. "We do not ram buses onto unsuspecting pedestrians walking along a promenade enjoying the

sunshine. We do not stab innocent individuals to death for being of a different religion from ours" he continued, "and we certainly wouldn't dream of flying a plane full of innocent passengers into the twin towers or any other high rise building with a view to massacring as many people as possible".

Above all else, he continued "we are grateful to be living in America and to bring up our children in peace and security as proud and patriotic Americans".

My colleague is right. Christians who settle in American (or anywhere in Europe) assimilate and become a productive and integral part of the society they live in. They do not come with the baggage of an alternate higher religious authority to whom they owe allegiance. Their loyalty is undivided and it goes unequivocally to their new host nations.

For those reasons, any ban on immigration from Muslim countries must exclude the Christians with whom we share our Judeo-Christian heritage. If we in the West continue to need immigrants we must not only exclude Christians from any ban, we ought to proactively seek them and encourage them to come. They will continue to make a positive contribution to our societies.

APPENDIX I:
Recent Terror Attacks

Spanish terror attacks: Thursday August 17 2017

A terrorist ploughed a van into crowds, killing 13 people and injuring more than a hundred, in Barcelona's Las Ramblas in the afternoon.

Hours later, police shot dead five attackers wearing fake suicide vests after a second attack in Cambrils, a coastal town south of Barcelona.

London Bridge terror attack: June 3 2017

The London terror attack killed eight people and injured many others on London Bridge and in nearby Borough Market on Saturday June 3.

Three knifemen were shot dead by police after mowing down pedestrians the bridge and going on a killing spree at pubs and restaurants at 10pm.

Manchester terror attack: May 22 2017

The Manchester terror attack killed at least 22 people and injured 59 others at an Ariana Grande concert at Manchester Arena on Monday May 22.

A lone suicide bomber detonated explosives among teenage fans leaving the concert at 10.33pm.

Paris shooting: April 20 2017

A policeman was killed on the Champs Elysees in Paris in what is being treated as a terror-related attack.

ISIS have claimed responsibility for the killing, which comes just days before the French presidential election.

The gunman has been named in the media as Karim Cheurfi, a 39-year-old man who allegedly served 15 years in prison for three attempted murders.

The attacker was shot dead at the scene.

Stockholm attack: April 7 2017

Four people were killed and at least fifteen were injured when a man drove a truck down a busy shopping street. Akhmat Akilov, a failed asylum seeker from Uzbekistan, has confessed to the crime, his lawyer said.

The 39-year-old has allegedly admitted being a member of ISIS and told police investigators that he had "achieved what he set out to do".

Westminster attack: March 22 2017

London attacker Khalid Masood mowed down pedestrians on Westminster Bridge, killing two men and two women and injuring many others.

The knifeman crashed his car into the railings outside Parliament, got out and ran into New Palace Yard where he stabbed a brave police officer to death.

Masood was shot dead by armed police.

Louvre knife attack: February 3 2017

A knifeman was shot while trying to attack a group of soldiers guarding the Louvre in Paris on February 3.

The attacker reportedly cried 'Allahu Akbar' and drew a machete on the soldiers after being told he could not enter the Louvre Carrousel shopping centre with two backpacks.

Prime Minister Bernard Cazeneuve said the attack was "clearly of terrorist nature" but said that no explosives were found in the bags.

Berlin Christmas market attack: December 19 2016

Attacker Anis Amri drove a lorry into a packed Christmas market, killing 12 people and injuring more than 60, in Berlin.

Normandy church attack: Tuesday July 26 2016

Armed men slit the throat of a priest and took several others hostage after storming a church during mass in Normandy on Tuesday July 26.

Two armed men stormed a church in Saint-Etienne-du-Rouvray, a suburb of Rouen in northern France.

The attackers slit the throat of elderly priest Father Jacques Hamel and took four other people hostage. One of hostages is fighting for his life.

Police have now shot dead the attackers. Islamic State (ISIS) has claimed that the men were soldiers of their sick cause.

Attacks in Germany: July 2016

A doctor died after being shot in a Berlin hospital on Tuesday July 26 during the fifth horror attack in Germany in just over a week.

The string of violent attacks started when an axe man hacked passengers on a train in Wurzburg on Monday July 18.

A young Iranian-German gunman went on a deadly rampage in Munich on Friday July 22 after being inspired by far-right killer Anders Breivik.

In two separate attacks on Sunday July 24, a man blew himself up in Ansbach and a man killed a pregnant woman during a machete attack in Reutlingen.

Nice terror attack: July 14 2016

A terrorist in a lorry mowed down revellers who had just finished watching a firework display to mark Bastille Day in France.

The horrific rampage killed 84 people and injured hundreds of others on the promenade in the seaside town of Nice.

The attacker Mohamed Lahouaiej Bouhlel, a 41-year-old Tunisian-born French citizen, was shot dead by security forces.

Brussels bombings: March 22 2016

The Brussels bombings killed 32 people and wounded more than 300 other victims in a day of terror.

There were two suicide bombings at Brussels Airport and another bombing at a Metro station in the Belgium capital.

Paris attacks: November 13 2015

A series of terrifying attacks in Paris killed 130 victims and injured hundreds of others. It was the most deadly assault on French soil since World War II.

A suicide bombing at the Stade de France stadium were followed by more explosions and shootings at popular bars and restaurants in Paris.

Three gunmen also opened fire at Bataclan concert hall and killed spectators who were watching the Eagles of Death Metal perform.

Charlie Hebdo attack: January 7 2015

Two masked gunmen carried out a bloody terror attack on the French satirical weekly newspaper Charlie Hebdo in Paris.

Brothers Saïd and Chérif Kouachi killed 12 people during the lunchtime massacre at the Charlie Hebdo offices in the French capital.

A policewoman was killed a day later. On January 9, another terrorist killed four hostages at a Jewish supermarket.

Spanish terror attacks: Thursday August 17 2017

A terrorist ploughed a van into crowds, killing 13 people and injuring more than a hundred, in Barcelona's Las Ramblas in the afternoon.

Hours later, police shot dead five attackers wearing fake suicide vests after a second attack in Cambrils, a coastal town south of Barcelona.

APPENDIX II:

Quran Quotes

It is the same whether or not you forewarn them (the unbelievers) ers], they will have no faith" (2:6).

"Allah will mock them and keep them long in sin, blundering blindly along" (2:15).

A fire "whose fuel is men and stones" awaits them (2:24).

They will be "rewarded with disgrace in this world and with grievous punishment on the Day of Resurrection" (2:85).

"Allah's curse be upon the infidels!" (2:89).

"They have incurred Allah's most inexorable wrath. An ignominious punishment awaits [them]" (2:90).

"Allah is the enemy of the unbelievers" (2:98).

"The unbelievers among the People of the Book [Christians and Jews], and the pagans, resent that any blessing should have been sent down to you from your Lord" (2:105).

"They shall be held up to shame in this world and sternly punished in the hereafter" (2.114).

"Those to whom We [Allah] have given the Book, and who read it as it ought to be read, truly believe in it; those that deny it shall assuredly be lost" (2:122).

"[We] shall let them live awhile, and then shall drag them to the scourge of the Fire. Evil shall be their fate" (2.126).

"The East and the West are Allah's. He guides whom He will to a straight path" (2.142).

"Do not say that those slain in the cause of Allah are dead. They are alive, but you are not aware of them" (Z:TSq.).

"But the infidels who die unbelievers shall incur the curse of Allah, the angels, and all men. Under it they shall remain for ever; their punishment shall not be lightened, nor shall they be reprieved" (za6z).

"They shall sigh with remorse, but shall never come out of the Fire" (Za68).

"The unbelievers are like beasts which, call out to them as one may, can hear nothing but a shout and a cry. Deaf, dumb, and blind, they understand nothing" (za72).

"Theirs shall be a woeful punishment" (Z:a7S).

How steadfastly they seek the Fire! That is because Allah has revealed the Book with truth; those that disagree about it are in extreme schism" (z:T76

"Slay them wherever you find them. Drive them out of the places from which they drove you. Idolatry

*is worse than carnage. [I]f they attack you put them
to the sword. Thus shall the unbelievers be rewarded:
but if they desist, Allah is forgiving and merciful.
Fight against them until idolatry is no more and
Allah's religion reigns supreme. But if they desist,
fight none except the evil doers"(za9o-93).*

*"Fighting is obligatory for you, much as you dis-
like it. But you may hate a thing although it is good
for you, and love a thing although it is bad for you.
Allah knows, but you know not" (z:zz6).*

*"They will not cease to fight against you until they
force you to renounce your faith-if they are able. But
whoever of you recants and dies an unbeliever, his
works shall come to nothing in this world and in the
world to come. Such men shall be the tenants of Hell,
wherein they shall abide forever. Those that have
embraced the Faith, and those that have fled their
land and fought for the cause of Allah, may hope for
Allah's mercy" (z:zy-a8).*

"Allah does not guide the evil-doers" (z:z58).

"Allah does not guide the unbelievers" (z:z6q.).

*"The evil-doers shall have none to help them"
(z:z7o).*

"Allah gives guidance to whom He will" (z:z7z).

"Those that deny Allah's revelations shall be sternly punished; Allah is mighty and capable of revenge" (3:5).

"As for the unbelievers, neither their riches nor their children will in the least save them from Allah's judgment. They shall become fuel for the Fire" (3ao).

"Say to the unbelievers: 'You shall be overthrown and driven into Hell-an evil resting place!'" (3az).

"The only true faith in Allah's sight is Islam. He that denies Allah's revelations should know that swift is Allah's reckoning" (3:z9).

"Let the believers not make friends with infidels in preference to the faithful-he that does this has nothing to hope for from Allah-except in self-defence" (3:z8).

"Believers, do not make friends with any but your own people. They will spare no pains to corrupt you. They desire nothing but your ruin. Their hatred is evident from what they utter with their mouths, but greater is the hatred which their breasts conceal" (3:na8).

"If you have suffered a defeat, so did the enemy. We alternate these vicissitudes among mankind so that Allah may know the true believers and choose martyrs from among you (Allah does not love the *evil-doers); and that Allah may test the faithful and annihilate the infidels" (3a4o).*

"Believers, if you yield to the infidels they will drag you back to unbelief and you will return headlong to perdition. We will put terror into the hearts of the unbelievers. The Fire shall be their home" (3:149-51).

"Believers, do not follow the example of the infidels, who say of their brothers when they meet death abroad or in battle: 'Had they stayed with us they would not have died, nor would they have been killed.' Allah will cause them to regret their words. If you should die or be slain in the cause of Allah, Allah's forgiveness and His mercy would surely be better than all the riches they amass" (3:156).

"Never think that those who were slain in the cause of Allah are dead. They are alive, and well provided for by their Lord; pleased with His gifts and rejoicing that those they left behind, who have not yet joined them, have nothing to fear or to regret; rejoicing in Allah's grace and bounty. Allah will not deny the faithful their reward" (3a6g).

"Let not the unbelievers think that We prolong their days for their own good. We give them respite only so that they may commit more grievous sins. Shameful punishment awaits them" (3a78).

"Those that suffered persecution for My sake and fought and were slain: I shall forgive them their sins and admit them to gardens watered by running streams, as a reward from Allah; Allah holds the richest recompense. Do not be deceived by the fortunes of the unbelievers in the land. Their prosperity is brief. Hell shall be their home, a dismal resting place" (3:195-96).

"Allah has cursed them in their unbelief" (4:46).

"Allah will not forgive those who serve other Allahs besides Him; but He will forgive whom He will for other sins. He that serves other Allahs besides Allah is guilty of a heinous sin. Consider those to whom a portion of the Scriptures was given. They believe in idols and false Allahs and say of the infidels: 'These are better guided than the believers'" (4:50-51).

"Those that deny Our revelation We will burn in fire. No sooner will their skins be consumed than We shall give them other skins, so that they may truly taste the scourge. Allah is mighty and wise" (4:55-56).

"Believers, do not seek the friendship of the infidels and those who were given the Book before you, who have made of your religion a jest and a pastime" (5:57).

"That which is revealed to you from your Lord will surely increase the wickedness and unbelief of many among them. We have stirred among them enmity and hatred, which will endure till the Day of Resurrection" (5:65).

"Allah does not guide the unbelievers" (5:67).

"That which is revealed to you from your Lord will surely increase the wickedness and unbelief of many among them. But do not grieve for the unbelievers" (5:69).

"You see many among them making friends with unbelievers. Evil is that to which their souls prompt them. They have incurred the wrath of Allah and shall endure eternal torment. You will find that the most implacable of men in their enmity to the faithful are the Jews and the pagans, and that the nearest in affection to them are those who say: 'We are Christians" (5:80-82).

"[T]hose that disbelieve and deny Our revelations shall become the inmates of Hell" (5:86).

"[T]hey deny the truth when it is declared to them: but they shall learn the consequences of their scorn" (6:5).

"We had made them more powerful in the land than yourselves [the Meccans], sent down for them

*abundant water from the sky and gave them rivers
that rolled at their feet. Yet because they sinned We
destroyed them all and raised up other generations
after them. If We sent down to you a Book inscribed
on real parchment and they touched it with their own
hands, the unbelievers would still assert: 'This is but
plain sorcery.' They ask: 'Why has no angel been sent
down to him [Muhammad]?' If We had sent down an
angel, their fate would have been sealed and they
would have never been reprieved" (6:5-8).*

*"Who is more wicked than the man who invents
falsehoods about Allah or denies His revelations?"
(6:2z).*

*"Some of them listen to you. But We have cast
veils over their hearts and made them hard of hearing
lest they understand your words. They will believe in
none of Our signs, even if they see them one and all.
When they come to argue with you the unbelievers
say: 'This is nothing but old fictitious tales.' They
forbid it and depart from it. They ruin none but
themselves, though they do not perceive it. If you
could see them when they are set before the Fire!
They will say: 'Would that we could return! Then we
would not deny the revelations of our Lord and would
be true believers' (6:23-27).*

"But if they were sent back, they would return to that which they have been forbidden. They are liars all" (6:29).

"Had Allah pleased He would have given them guidance, one and all" (6:35).

"Deaf and dumb are those that deny Our revelations: they blunder about in darkness. Allah confounds whom He will, and guides to a straight path whom He pleases." (6:39)

"[T]heir hearts were hardened, and Satan made their deeds seem fair to them. And when they had clean forgotten Our admonition We granted them all that they desired; but just as they were rejoicing in what they were given, We suddenly smote them and they were plunged into utter despair. Thus were the evil-doers annihilated. Praise be to Allah, Lord of the Universe!" (6:q.3-45).

"Those that deny Our revelations shall be punished for their misdeeds" (6:q.9).

"Such are those that are damned by their own sins. They shall drink scalding water and be sternly punished for their unbelief" (6:70).

"Could you but see the wrongdoers when death overwhelms them! With hands outstretched, the angels will say: 'Yield up your souls. You shall be

rewarded with the scourge of shame this day, for you have said of Allah what is untrue and scorned His revelations" (6:93).

"Avoid the pagans. Had Allah pleased, they would not have worshipped idols. We will turn away their hearts and eyes from the Truth since they refused to believe in it at first. We will let them blunder about in their wrongdoing. If We sent the angels down to them, and caused the dead to speak to them,. and ranged all things in front of them, they would still not believe, unless Allah willed otherwise. Thus have We assigned for every prophet an enemy: the devils among men and jinn, who inspire each other with vain and varnished falsehoods. But had your Lord pleased, they would not have done so. Therefore leave them to their own inventions, so that the hearts of those who have no faith in the life to come may be inclined to what they say and, being pleased, persist in their sinful ways" (6ao7-iz).

"The devils will teach their votaries to argue with you. If you obey them you shall yourselves become idolaters. Allah will humiliate the transgressors and mete out to them a grievous punishment for their scheming" (6azi-25).

"If Allah wills to guide a man, He opens his bosom to Islam. But if he pleases to confound him, He makes his bosom small and narrow as though he

were climbing up to heaven. Thus shall Allah lay the scourge on the unbelievers" (6a25).

By the same author

Nation Building in Islamic Society

Publisher: Pen Press (16 April 2014)
Language: English

Michael's first book, Nation Building in Islam was originally written as his PhD thesis. It is a fascinating study of how most Arab leaders created functioning states but failed to establish cohesive nations. Michael revisited the book four years ago and decided that now was the time to put it into the public domain.

Armed with the West's blueprint, can the Islamic world leapfrog a lengthy historical process and achieve in a few decades what the West took centuries to accomplish? So far all indications point the other way. The mind set of Islamists, literalists and their sympathisers is rooted in the sixth century. Democracy starts with the deliverance of the individual and its foundation lies in the family, the building bloc of the nation. Nation Building is the ultimate endeavour in a lengthy road map beginning with "Man Building". Here the West has succeeded in vanquishing the scourge of patriarchy and the medieval culture of machismo. It has established equality between men and women, a far cry from today's reality in the Islamic world where the culture of shame (AAR & EIB), honour (SHARAF mostly as related to females' sexual life), and HARAM (as forbidden by Allah) reigns supreme. The Region, in its current Islamic year of 1434 AH Hijri, is on the eve of the very same convulsions and seismic changes that began to sweep the West in and before the same year of 1434 AD.

The Maskmaker

Publisher: Pen Press (6 Nov. 2010)

Language: English

ISBN-10: 1907499784

Michael's love of writing has also extended to fiction. He wrote a novel, The Maskmaker which was published to considerable acclaim in 2012. Part fact, part fiction, it was based on his personal experiences of life in LA during the early 1990's. The easy divorce society in which he lived at that time and the resulting casual destruction of family life was so alien to his upbringing. An unusual and complex novel of two couples' lives, love and deception woven into an interesting story.

Ira's story is shocking. LA's most eligible bachelor and successful businessman in Hollywood's glamorous motion picture industry, has everything he wants– then he meets Martha. Across the Atlantic, Alex tells his uncannily similar story as he finds

himself totally unmasked by the woman he loves –
Cathy.

A drama of tangled relationships unravels…Both
Ira and Alex are united by a common bond of
experience – both caught up in intricate webs of sex,
lies and deceit, both women wearing the mask of
pretence concealing their true identities and past.

Engaging, frank, sensitive, and even heart-
breaking, the Maskmaker s tale is compulsive
reading.